Plantations of Virginia

Plantations of Virginia

Jai Williams and Charlene Giannetti

Globe Pequot

Guilford, Connecticut

Globe Pequot

An imprint of Rowman & Littlefield

Distributed by NATIONAL BOOK NETWORK

British Library Cataloguing in Publication Information available

Library of Congress Cataloging-in-Publication Data

Names: Williams, Jai (Photographer), author, photographer. | Giannetti, Charlene C., author.
Title: Plantations of Virginia / Jai Williams and Charlene Giannetti.
Description: Guilford, Connecticut : Globe Pequot, 2017. | Includes index. |
Description based on print version record and CIP data provided by publisher; resource not viewed.
Identifiers: LCCN 2016030195 (print) | LCCN 2016028801 (ebook) | ISBN 9781493024803 (e-book) |
ISBN 9781493024797 (pbk.)
Subjects: LCSH: Plantations—Virginia—Guidebooks. | Historic buildings—Virginia—Guidebooks. | Architecture—Virginia—Guidebooks. | Virginia—Tours.

Classification: LCC F227 (print) | LCC F227 .W67 2017 (ebook) | DDC
917.5504/44—dc23
LC record available at https://lccn.loc.gov/2016030195

Printed in the United States of America

Contents

Preface

The advertisements say that "Virginia is for Lovers," but as new arrivals to the state, we found that Virginia is also for history lovers. Old Dominion, the nickname earned from being the first British colony on the mainland, overflows with stories. Jamestown was the first settlement in the New World. The colony saw battles during the American Revolution, and during the Civil War Virginia found itself the epicenter of that conflict. Due to the state's dependence on agriculture, slavery became critical to its economy. Virginia seceded from the union on April 17, 1861, after the Battle of Fort Sumter and on April 24 joined the Confederate States of America. Richmond would become the Confederacy's capital.

Also known as the "Mother of Presidents," Virginia has produced eight presidents, more than any other state. And three of those presidents—George Washington, Thomas Jefferson, and James Madison—were Founding Fathers whose leadership and inspiration were critical to the birth and success of the new country. Their homes—Mount Vernon, Monticello, and Montpelier, respectively—remain the jewels in the crown and should be experienced by every American for their historical value.

We arrived in Virginia by different routes. Charlene, a New Yorker, took a second home in Alexandria in March 2012, while Jai moved from Dallas, Texas, in April 2008 to further her education and career. Charlene, a journalist, author, and editor, is the cofounder and editor of the award-winning website Woman Around Town. Jai, a writer and recognized photographer, is one of Woman Around Town's contributors. In conversations, we discovered we shared a fascination with Virginia's history and specifically the state's plantations, which number more than 40. Living near Mount Vernon, we had visited Washington's home many times. But soon we began to branch out, learning about the many other plantations sprinkled throughout the state. Each one had a story to tell.

We spent six months traveling around Virginia, taking tours, talking with those tasked with caring for these properties. A handful are tourist destinations and have professional staffs. Others are works-in-progress, in the midst of costly renovations. Like so many areas of our country, Virginia has become focused on preserving its history, which, in many cases, includes saving and restoring these homes and the surrounding grounds.

A few of these plantations remain in private hands, families raising their children surrounded by history. Many are still working farms, raising crops to bring in revenue. A handful have been converted to bed-and-breakfasts so that visitors can soak up history while they relax in comfortable surroundings. Some are now managed by the National Park Service, while others have been acquired by local organizations that continue to care for them and raise funds for their upkeep.

Each plantation required research. We gathered information from official sources, including the National Register of Historic Places, the plantation websites and written materials they provided, and from the oral tours given by each plantation's staff or volunteers. At times we found what was recited on tours conflicted with the information we gathered from other sources. Each plantation reviewed what we wrote, and accommodations were made to ensure the information was as accurate as possible.

We discovered that slavery remains a controversial topic. While some plantations are committed to telling the full story of their history, others were not so forthcoming. Several plantations have exhibits on their slave history and continue to collect information from descendants. In some ways, what we encountered during our travels mirrors what's happening in our country, which continues to grapple with the legacy of slavery.

We hope that we will inspire you to travel to Virginia and walk in our shoes, visiting some of the plantations that we write about. Because many are located in clusters, one trip will allow visits to several, each one unique.

This journey has been one of enlightenment and excitement. We want to thank all the people who spent time with us while we gathered information. We were overwhelmed by their commitment to preserving this very important part of our nation's history. Their enthusiasm was infectious, and we hope we have conveyed those feelings with each story in this book.

—Jai Williams and Charlene Giannetti

History as Seen through the Plantations of Virginia

As the first colony settled by England in the New World, Virginia's landscape has changed over the course of its quadricentennial history. From the indigenous people to the wave of colonists and slaves that came afterward, together they built a foundation for shaping America into what we know it as today.

Agricultural growth boosted the population of the infant territory. Plantations contributed significantly, providing commercial revenue through the planting, harvesting, and selling of goods by either indentured or enslaved labor. With over 40 plantations scattered throughout Virginia, this book's purpose is to highlight some of those homes before their stories are lost in time. Both privately and publicly owned and operated, many of these homes' livelihoods peaked during the 18th, 19th, and 20th centuries, often witnessing some of the most memorable events in history. Within these stories, points will be mentioned highlighting military history, familial lineages, architecture, economics, and slave life. Nevertheless, each home's restoration progress is just as noteworthy, as preservation and discovery are important for the next generation.

ARCHITECTURE

Depending on the time of construction, wealth contributed heavily to the plantation home's assembly, with a hierarchical structure placed not only on its owners, but on the house itself. Colonists who were able to create a prosperous market for themselves had the ability to splurge. Plantation homes made of brick were considered the crème de la crème, as having enough capital to employ a brick mason among other craftsmen was a luxury. In contrast, those built of wood were deemed not as upscale but were just as coveted, since most of the population lived in much smaller, cramped one-room structures.

Architectural details reflected the style throughout each home. Ranging from Georgian to Federal to Neoclassical to Greek Revival, each design impacted aspects like symmetry and space. Many structures were shaped after those in Europe, especially England, but architects also developed their own style and were heavily influenced by Roman and Greek architecture. It is said that Roman architect Vitruvius Pollio identified three aspects in constructing a well-built structure: *firmitas*, *utilitas*, and *venustas*. This translates into *firmitas*—strength, *utilitas*—purpose of utility, and *venustas*—aesthetics. In Henry Wotton's 1624 *Principles of Architecture*, he eloquently states those conditions interpret as firmness, commodity, and delight.

In Virginia, these three aspects are particularly evident due to the wealth of its upper class from the Atlantic Ocean's coastline to the Chesapeake Bay's inland waterways. Compared to its New England counterparts, Southern Colonial architecture differed due to great halls where guests were greeted, rooms for entertaining placed on the first floor such as a parlor, dining room, or family room. Furthermore, massive chimneys, sometimes numbering upward of eight, of various colors and shapes of brickwork, along with designated river and carriage entryways, could be found on certain plantation homes. With the amount of land many planters owned, outer buildings also showcased their wealth. Icehouses, stables, laundry, kitchens (winter and summer), and overseer and slave quarters all had to be built to support the plantation's livelihood. However, it is important to note the Southern Colonial style began to change as homes were built farther down the Eastern Seaboard and in the Deep South.

With each home, a large team—architect, builder, craftsmen, and indentured servants and/or slaves—were needed to execute the owner's vision. Structures requiring the least amount of work could take between 2 and 4 years, while others were extremely labor-intensive, commanding 5 to 10 years, with the most extreme cases taking 15. What may take 30 to 45 minutes to tour took years to build at the sacrifice of those involved in the process. Nevertheless, there is something breathtaking about each one. With their individual quirks and prideful stateliness, secrets of the past are laid at your feet, inviting you to cross the threshold. Or in this case, through the digestion of each page read.

FAMILIAL LINEAGE

Virginia has many nicknames, including "Old Dominion," "Mother of Presidents," and "Mother of Statesmen," to name a few. Referred to as a dominion because of its loyalty to the crown of England as well as being a place of sovereignty within the colonies, "Old Dominion" is one of Virginia's most beloved names. "Mother of Presidents" stems from the fact it is the only state to have produced eight American presidents since the colonies won their independence in 1776. "Mother of Statesmen" makes reference to the countless number of men who provided service to the colony and later the construction of America's democratic ideology. Virginia reached statehood in 1788, the 10th among the colonies to do so.

Familial lineage determined the difference between a life of luxury and one of poverty. Prominent names such as Washington, Jefferson, Lee, Randolph, Carter, and Berkeley held their weight in gold, as those lucky enough to be born or married into "Virginia royalty" were guaranteed a lifestyle many could only imagine. Furthermore, wealth provided the ability to participate in civil activities, governmental affairs, and commercial trade. Capital made from these endeavors was spent on commodities like exotic spices, fine china, elaborate furnishings, paintings, and more. With such extravagances displayed for guests to marvel at and enjoy, many of these families welcomed not only dignitaries and military personnel into their home, but also, depending on their location, curious and wayward travelers. To keep theft at bay, valuable items were kept under lock and key or under the watchful eye of the lady of the house.

Arranged marriages weren't uncommon for those in the agricultural ruling class. As the wealthiest families continued to enlarge their acreage, slaves, and possessions, each marriage was considered a business arrangement to preserve the greater good of separatism. Yet there were instances in which couples of the gentry class did marry for love, one example being Benjamin Harrison IV and Anne Carter, who were from two of the colony's most affluent families.

After the Civil War, an uprising among the middle class occurred, while fighting the North depleted most of the well-to-do families' resources in the South. Although some were able to recover, many were never able to do so, choosing instead to start over. A number of homes were abandoned, allowing the grandeur of the structures to diminish during the late 19th and early 20th centuries. Later on, untold secrets would be discovered by each new owner.

ECONOMICS

Colonial life was extremely difficult. While husbands managed the books, bought and traded slaves, selected the crops to be grown, and participated in civic duties, the wives, even those in a position of prominence, were expected to bear hordes of children, most importantly a male heir to inherit

the family's wealth. Two hundred years before women's suffrage, a Colonial woman's lot in life was to take care of all of the domestic aspects of the plantation. This ranged from instructing enslaved house servants and rearing children to keeping track of supplies and entertaining guests. Together the couple would be expected to operate a successful agricultural business.

The economic environment differed throughout the centuries, specifically during the 17th century, when King William I forged a partnership with rich London investors to form a joint venture called the Virginia Company. In the beginning, the company expected its return in gold and silver, but after little success and the demise of large numbers of colonists due to disease and Indian attacks, investors turned to other means, including tobacco. However, by the time tobacco cultivation profitably commenced, the Indian Massacre of 1622 occurred, killing about a quarter of the population of Jamestown. In 1624 King William I turned Virginia into a royal colony, completely under his control. Land acquisition and ownership symbolized wealth, access, and the ability to vote within the governing body, the House of Burgesses.

In the late 17th century, the Crown started to demand capital through passing various acts and stringent taxation. These new laws upset many colonists who, having lived with little interference from the Crown for over a century, felt they were no longer British, and they coined a newfangled term, American. This led to the American Revolution and later independence. As the newfound country decided on its future, economics in the 18th century solely revolved around regional prosperity—New England with its shipping industry, the middle colonies with their timber and fur trapping, and the southern colonies with their rice and tobacco cultivation. The main resource throughout each region was land.

Up until the Civil War, agriculture reigned supreme. Northern cities began to delve into industrialism due to their strategic location along various rivers, which perpetuated the steam needed for a modernized economy. After the Civil War, the South was heavily hit, as its way of life completely shifted from one of prosperity to one of destitution. The North, however, was able to maintain its comfortable ways. Because of this, a number of plantation homes suffered greatly as a result of the large amount of capital needed for their upkeep. With the great wave of immigration, people from other countries in addition to those from other states took advantage of the homes in foreclosure, changing their aesthetic along with it. Few homes remained in their previous original form.

A photograph of Shirley Plantation taken by William Henry Jackson (1843–1942) in the early 1900s

The Atlantic slave trade was one of the most lucrative human-trafficking ventures known to man and is well documented. It began as early as the 15th century for European and Muslim traders but didn't become widespread until the 17th century, when European countries commenced numerous exploratory expeditions to grow their wealth. It is estimated that 12 million people were sold or forced into slavery, with 10.5 million landing in North and South America, many in what is now known as the Caribbean and Brazil. Those sent to North America, particularly Virginia, were fewer in number but the first to experience persecution and degradation for centuries to come.

Before slavery became a means for some men to achieve wealth, another option was indentured servitude. A person would agree to work as a laborer or apprentice for a certain period of time, most often 5 to 7 years. Depending on the arrangement, a servant's passage could either be paid or unpaid, wages earned or worked off; however, normally at the end of one's service, freedom would be granted. Furthermore, a small stipend known as "freedom dues" was usually given or some type of payment of land, crops, or weaponry.

The difference between enslaved Africans and indentured servants was the utilization of choice. Although some blacks were indentured slaves and received their freedom, many did not. During the early 17th century, those blacks fortunate enough to be free were able to own land, honor their civic duties, and in some cases marry outside their race; however, as indentured servants became less available, the reliance on African enslaved labor intensified. This inspired the white ruling class to begin a systematic change and identification of race.

With the Virginia Slave Laws, the latter part of the 17th century became increasingly difficult for blacks with any hope of freedom. Laws implemented from the 1640s through the 1660s signified a shift from indentured servitude to permanent enslavement. Later, the laws from the 1660s to 1680 outlined how those who owned enslaved people were to treat, acknowledge, and punish them, with a heavy reliance on differences between each race. But from 1680 to 1705, the laws took a dark turn toward separation, humiliation, legal recourse, and most importantly, death.

At any given time, slaves outnumbered their white counterparts on a plantation. And though slave rebellions occurred, only a handful were successful. Those slaves that didn't succeed were prosecuted to the fullest extent of the law to act as an example to prevent other revolts. These constricting rulings and executions set the tone for two centuries of suppression and fear.

After the Civil War, the Reconstruction period (1865–1877) witnessed the addition of the 14th, 15th, and 16th amendments to the Constitution guaranteeing basic human rights such as the abolishment of slavery, due process requirements, and the right to vote. Nevertheless, the South implemented a new set of edicts known as the Black Codes between 1865 and 1866 limiting the freedom of newly freed slaves and their economic ascent. By the late 19th and early 20th centuries, Jim Crow laws enforced by local and state governments further stifled black opportunity until the Civil Rights Act of 1964.

Regardless of which side a person experienced, plantation homes throughout Virginia carried out and bore witness to a number of these legal encounters as slaves took care of everyday life from planting, tending, and harvesting crops to domestic tasks involving the plantation family (washing, cooking, and so on). Because of this, slaves were an integral part of numerous plantations' financial success, especially when war broke out during the country's infancy.

MILITARY ACTION

Up until the Revolutionary War of 1776, most of the skirmishes fought on the New World's soil concerned American Indians and foreign territories. Involvement in those wars provided colonists a newfound sense of confidence to challenge the Crown for their own progression. The plantations housed many of the families who commanded, fought, or provided some type of assistance to America's military history. The four major wars reflecting this involvement are the Anglo-Powhatan Wars (1609–1614 and 1622–1626), the Revolutionary War (1765–1783), the War of 1812 (1812–1815), and the Civil War (1861–1865). Four more major wars were fought after the aforementioned, but by then the descent of agricultural life surrounding plantations had dissipated as industrialization spurred citizens to seek better opportunities in urban cities.

As previously pointed out, Virginian colonists had a tense relationship with the various Native American tribes located along the Eastern Seaboard, specifically those from the Powhatan Confederacy, also known as Virginia Algonquians. Massacres ensued on both sides, which made it almost impossible for colonists to live outside of the protective forts. Yet as more colonists traveled to the New World, they quickly outnumbered and overpowered Indians in the area. No longer considered a direct threat, those landowners who had enough capital to build homes did so as a way to illustrate their nouveau wealth.

On the heels of the French and Indian War, those who called America home decided that a foreign hand in their matters wasn't needed. Most of the battles were fought throughout New England, and the South, particularly Virginia, didn't see action until much later. The Declaration of Independence was adopted on July 4, 1776; however, it wasn't until October 19, 1781, that General George Washington's Continental army alongside the French defeated British General Lord Charles Cornwallis at Yorktown, Virginia, which ended the Revolutionary War.

England, however, continued to engage in warfare. While British and French troops vied for control of trade waterways, each attempted to block the United States from doing so with the other. Recently formed, the United States had something to prove, or should we say, maintain. Due to Virginia's strategic location along the Atlantic Ocean, British naval ships began to once again terrorize the state's coastline, prompting James Madison to ask Congress to declare war, the first president to do so. Several other prominent Virginians were also a part of the war, which came to be known as the War of 1812, including Virginia royalty such as James Monroe, William Henry Harrison, and James Barbour.

Later in the 19th century, with the Civil War literally exploding all around, many Virginia plantations were occupied either by Confederate or Union troops. Nowhere else in the South were plantations so affected by the nation's bloodiest war than in Virginia. At times, families fled, leaving behind slaves to manage and care for the properties. Upon their return, many planters lost everything, including their opulent homes.

RENOVATION

Well into the 20th century, most of these dilapidated homes waited patiently until private or public ownership resulted. Those that are privately owned are sometimes open to the public for special occasions, such as Virginia's annual Garden Week during the month of April. The renovation and upkeep of homes that are publicly operated, either by historical societies or government associations, is a challenge. From paint analysis to furniture refurbishment to structural reinforcement, each home is a different beast to tackle.

An 1861 lithograph of George Washington's home, Mount Vernon, showing the dwelling, grounds, and outbuildings with tourists in the foreground

For those who live in Virginia, participation in the various membership clubs is welcomed. Many of the clubs offer special events including dinners, distinguished guest speakers, and the ability to see and enjoy these homes in all of their glory, something difficult to achieve in a 30- to 60-minute tour. Yet it is understood that not everyone lives in Old Dominion, so other means of revenue are garnered from visitors, like through gift shops. Supportive of one another, many clubs provide information about other plantations in the surrounding area.

Some plantations have gone as far as to enact scenes from the past, which are a huge part of the educational experience not only for students but for anyone interested in days gone by. Fortunately many still operate as a source of agriculture, leasing their land to either tenant farmers or businesses. Some have become recognized bed-and-breakfasts, while others provide destination weddings. If the possibility arises to visit any of these mentioned homes, do so. Despite the fact that the 21st century's obsession with modernization is slowly encroaching upon these plantations, all is not lost.

While walking through the house, listen carefully. It speaks whether by creaking, squeaking, or sometimes allowing one to capture a glimpse of something that suddenly disappears with the blink of an eye. Realize that some of these homes have survived four centuries of changes, with familial generations passing along their history to the next. Tears were shed within the walls or along their grounds either from the pain of loss or joyousness of gain. Nevertheless, their stories are intricate pieces contributing to America's historical account. The resilience of these plantations homes is inspiring, as no matter where they've ended up by today's standards, they're still standing, commanding the respect of their tenants and guests.

Northern Virginia

Less than 30 minutes from the nation's capital with one-third of the state's population, Northern Virginia's prime location makes it a pivotal place. Many of Virginia's first families moved here wanting to be closer to the political action in the federal city or to participate in its bustling trade scene. While travelers once journeyed by horse and carriage, Northern Virginia is now a transportation center, with two airports, Ronald Reagan and Dulles, and a Metro system linking suburban Maryland and Virginia to Washington, DC. Other attractions include Arlington National Cemetery and Great Falls National Park. The federal government has a presence with the Pentagon, the Central Intelligence Agency, and the Patent and Trademark Office, all located in the area. George Washington's Mount Vernon can be reached after a scenic drive along the Potomac River down the George Washington Memorial Parkway. The first president's home is the best known and most visited plantation in Virginia, attracting tourists from all over the world.

Northern Virginia saw much action during the Civil War, and historic sites continue to draw crowds, including Old Town Alexandria, once occupied by the Union army and now a residential area whose past has been well preserved, from the cobblestone streets to the stately homes, many dating back to the 1700s. In addition to Mount Vernon, we cover six other plantations in this chapter: Chatham Manor, Ellwood Manor, Gunston Hall, Liberia Plantation, Sully Historic Site, and Woodlawn Plantation.

Chatham Manor

120 Chatham Lane
Fredericksburg, VA 22405
(540) 371-0802
www.nps.gov/frsp

A VANTAGE POINT COMPOUNDED BY WAR

Before Chatham Manor became a strategic lookout point during the Civil War, it was considered an opulent home. Like most of the homes built in the 18th century, its Georgian composition is noticeable as the 180-foot-long bricked mansion sits perfectly perched above the Rappahannock River. Chatham has survived throughout the centuries, from its prerevolutionary construction by William Fitzhugh to its current ownership by the National Park Service. From a plantation to a historic landmark, Chatham commands your respect as it is one of the only great houses left along the river's bank.

Chatham's first owner, William Fitzhugh, was no stranger to the area. Son of Lucy Carter (daughter of Robert "King" Carter) and the great-grandson of Colonel William Fitzhugh, William Fitzhugh was of considerable financial stature, as his family was instrumental in developing both Stafford and King George Counties during the 17th and 18th centuries. When he came of age, he married Ann Randolph, daughter of Colonel Peter Randolph, and together they inherited Colonel Fitzhugh's generous bounty.

A friend of George Washington's, William served in the House of Burgesses from 1772 until 1775, shortly before the fevered uptick of the Revolutionary War. Throughout the war he continued to contribute politically, first as a delegate of the Second Continental Congress in 1776 and later in the senate for four years from 1781 to 1785. An avid horse racer and later a breeder, Fitzhugh was more than a political force. He and Ann enjoyed entertaining their many visitors, including George Washington and Thomas Jefferson. Guests alternated from presidential candidates to those of high society. It is said that the number of people that came to visit Chatham is one of the reasons the Fitzhughs moved to Alexandria.

As avid farmers and experimentalists, Fitzhugh and Washington shared a commonality deeper than politics. However, their plantations varied greatly. The Tidewater area of Virginia where Chatham is located is known for its marshes and low-lying plains, covering territories from the Potomac River down to the James River. Tobacco, an important crop for the region, wasn't so much responsible for the agricultural success of Chatham. William chose to grow wheat and corn, experimenting with different strains, some even provided by his good friend George. This fact is nowhere more evident than the presence of a gristmill built to accommodate the amount of grain being produced.

John Hennessy, chief historian for the Fredericksburg and Spotsylvania National Military Park in Fredericksburg, Virginia, has written two books on Civil War battles and has studied the history of slavery on the two plantations he oversees, Chatham Manor and Ellwood Manor. He shares the following:

The physical prominence of Chatham, the bounty served at its tables, and the congenial hospitality enjoyed in its halls reflected the lofty prominence of its pre–Civil War owners. But the refined veneer obscured a hard fact: none of it was possible without the labor of enslaved people.

The caviar that graced the tables at Chatham was harvested by slaves from the sturgeon in the Rappahannock River. The elegant buggies: driven by slaves. William Fitzhugh's famous prize-winning racehorses: ridden to victory by slaves. The fruit for the brandy, the shoes for the horses, the wool from the sheep, the crops for market—all of them the work and responsibility of slaves. The leisure to never worry about a bedpan or chamber pot, to never build a fire or wash a dish, or perhaps even to never change a baby's diaper—leisure provided white owners and visitors only by the presence of slaves. For its white residents and visitors, Chatham was often a pleasing, memorable retreat. For Chatham's slaves, it more closely resembled a factory village or work camp.

Probably at no time prior to 1865 did the white residents of Chatham amount to more than 20% of the total population of the place, and usually far less than that. The slave population at Chatham fluctuated between 40 and 110 and included an array of tradesmen and artisans that not only provided for the needs of Chatham, but, by being hired out, helped keep Chatham's owners in cash: carpenters, a tanner, blacksmiths, a jockey, cooks. These people had no legal names. Their marriages were not legally recognized; births and deaths were not recorded; their burial places unmarked and forgotten. Today, we often know of them because they, like buggies and horses and jewelry and tools, appeared in the inventory of a will, paired with a dollar value and, perhaps, a note on their virtues or limitations as a laborer. "Gowen Bessee, a Carpenter, aged 45, $300"; "Dick (tanner) aged 50, $200." Or "Negro Man Bently (a cripple) $0."

Within this world—a world controlled sometimes with violence or the threat of separation—slaves forged a distinct society of faith, community, and (when allowed by their owners) family. And within this world, enslaved people struggled for freedom. Most often they did not seek absolute freedom, but rather time and space within the bonds of slavery. Occasionally, they rebelled. At Chatham just after New Year's Day in 1805, a group of slaves objected to being ordered back to work before they had finished their holiday celebrations. They attacked the overseer, and when he ran for help, they attacked the help too. In the end, one white responder and two slaves died that day. A third slave was hanged ("a sufficient example to the others," wrote one white man), and two others were sold south.

Only war ultimately shattered the restraints of slavery at Chatham and elsewhere. The end of slavery meant the end of Chatham as it had been. Over the coming decades, without the labor to work them, Chatham's farmlands were sold off, until the estate amounted to just a couple dozen acres. From a prominent, expansive place of production, Chatham transformed to a secluded refuge atop a riverside hill.

To this day, when walking Chatham's grounds, it's hard not to imagine its expansive peach, apple, and pear orchards, planted fields, and plentiful livestock. With outer buildings surrounding the manor including an icehouse, a mill, a blacksmith's shop, and fisheries, among other desirable features, Chatham showcased the Fitzhughs' wealth. However, today only three of the original structures remain.

From 1806 until 1857 Chatham changed hands five times, beginning with Major Churchill Jones, who bought the house from Fitzhugh for a sum of $20,000. Major Jones willed it to his

brother William Jones, who sold it to John Coalter, who willed it to his wife Hannah Coalter, who gave it to her daughter. However, Mrs. Coalter's daughter wasn't as tied to the home as previous owners had been and auctioned off Chatham to the highest bidder in 1857. The new homeowners just so happened to be Hannah's half-sister Betty Churchill Jones Lacy and husband J. Horace Lacy.

In her will, Hannah Coalter had asked that the 95 slaves be granted their freedom and sent to Liberia (West Africa) to live the rest of their lives. Unfortunately, Mr. Lacy was a staunch supporter of slavery and went to court over the matter. Since slaves were regarded as property, not people, the deceased Mrs. Coalter's wishes were overturned.

The Lacys enjoyed their beautiful home for three years before the Civil War started, but as the topic of slavery continued to circle throughout the South, it became clear that something was bound to happen. The Lacys owned another property across the Rappahannock but did not take refuge there, as fighting was expected to occur heavily throughout the area. So Mrs. Lacy and the children left as soon as Union soldiers arrived, while Mr. Lacy signed up for the Confederacy to serve as a staff officer.

Chatham played a vital role in the Civil War, though perhaps not as the Lacys had envisioned. Upon their leaving, under the leadership of General Irvin McDowell, about 30,000 Union troops occupied the home until the war's end, as Chatham's vantage point was perfect for keeping an eye on the Confederate troops stationed in Fredericksburg, directly across the river. President Abraham Lincoln visited McDowell and his men, making the manor one of the few to have three presidents stop over: Washington, Jefferson, and Lincoln.

But the fighting had just begun. A tactical military highlight on Chatham's grounds was the first use of magnetic telegraphs on a battlefield. Famous names that served and descended upon the house during the war include acclaimed poet Walt Whitman, who assisted surgeons while looking for his brother Lieutenant George Whitman. Clara Barton, founder of the world-renowned American Red Cross, attended to Union battalions sprawled across the front lawn. With heavy casualties on both sides, the troops moved on to fight in new areas. When the Lacys returned in 1865, their beloved home was no longer fit to inhabit, and they moved 20 miles away to Ellwood Manor, their property across the Rappahannock.

The number of postbellum owners that called Chatham home were just as many as before the war. However, much credit is given to Brigade General Daniel B. Devore and his wife, Helen, who poured astronomical sums of money into the neglected home. American landscape architect Ellen Biddle Shipman, daughter of a Civil War general, designed more than 650 gardens in her career, but the beautiful gardens of Chatham are considered some of her best and can still be enjoyed today. With statues and graveled pavement, the east lawn reflects sunlight off of the dew-covered grass and plants. Trees that date to the 19th century seem to cover the exterior of the nine-room mansion like a cloak. Daniel Devore sold Chatham to John Lee Pratt, vice president of General Motors, in 1931; it was the last time the house would be in private ownership. In 1975 Pratt willed Chatham to the National Park Service, where it has remained.

Restoration has been a slow process, but Chatham's documentation is effectively detailed. Ghost stories are not uncommon, as the turmoil experienced by many left haunting spirits traipsing around. One such ghost is known as the "Lady in White," an upper-class Englishwoman from Colonial times. As the story goes, her parrot died and she fell in love with the taxidermist who tended to her pet. Her father, enraged with her class selection, sent her to live with William Fitzhugh in the colonies. The taxidermist followed her across the Atlantic to Chatham Manor, and the two were to run away together. On the night of their getaway, supposedly one of George Washington's soldiers was made aware of the plan and dutifully reported the news to the general. Upon the lady's descent from the second-story window to meet her lover, instead there stood the general himself. She returned to England and the unlucky taxidermist was left behind, not having enough money for a second passage. Although she married another, she vowed upon her deathbed to return to Chatham every seven years to walk the path to her beloved taxidermist. The manor's current staff commemorates her mournful journey, allowing visitors to walk in the footsteps of a brokenhearted lover.

From the riverbank Chatham remains a beacon of light, a reminder of Fredericksburg's and Spotsylvania's embattled past.

Ellwood Manor

36380 Constitution Highway
Orange, VA 22960
(703) 777-3174
www.fowb.org

BATTLE OF THE WILDERNESS

Five miles across the Rappahannock River from the palatial Chatham Manor is another manor called Ellwood. Once owned by William Jones, both homes fell under his care, as his brother Major Churchill Jones also owned Chatham, which was sold to him by William Fitzhugh. Constructed in 1790, Ellwood wasn't as ostentatious as its sister property, rather more of a farmhouse built to produce the necessary revenue for the Jones family.

Born in 1750, William and his brother moved from Middlesex County, Virginia, to Spotsylvania to pursue their fortune. Many of their peers considered the area wild and commonly referred to it as "the Wilderness." As previous occupants of tobacco fields had moved on to newer plots of land, the area the Jones brothers settled on had deep thickets and undergrowth. Clearing the land for a farm proved to be quite tedious, requiring the use of enslaved labor and animals as well as the simplest tools. What started as a 300-acre plantation grew into 5,000 acres at the height of its production.

Both brothers married their sweethearts, in William's case, Betty Churchill. They were married for 50 years and had one child; however, William outlived Betty, who died in 1823. At the age of 77, he married Betty's grandniece, Lucinda Gordon, who was only 16. This practice wasn't uncommon for the time, as property remaining in the family superseded any politically deemed correctness. William, spry in mind and body, fathered a daughter with Lucinda whom they named Betty Churchill Jones.

William Jones also owned a tavern a few miles away, which served as a source of income. Guests included the Marquis de Lafayette and supposedly James Monroe and James Madison. Jones was good friends with Henry "Light Horse Harry" Lee and housed the officer in one of Ellwood's bedrooms, where he wrote his memoirs on the Revolutionary War.

William Jones passed away in 1845 at 95. His will stated that as long as Lucinda Gordon Jones never remarried, Ellwood would stay in her possession. However, Lucinda remarried, and her daughter, Betty, inherited the almost 5,000 acres at the age of 17, making her one of the most eligible bachelorettes of her time. Betty met J. Horace Lacy at Eagle Point in Gloucester, Virginia, and they were married in October 1847 at Ellwood. Strong in will, Betty was matched by her husband's spirit. A staunch supporter of the Confederacy, he was pro-secession and became an officer during the Civil War.

Just a few feet from Ellwood's doorstep, the Battle of the Wilderness took place, thought to be where General Ulysses Grant's Union army began to gain an upper hand in the war with the start of the Overland Campaign. Extremely heavy fighting occurred all around the plantation, and while Mr. Lacy went off to fight in the war, Mrs. Lacy left with their children to a neighboring town.

Eleven Confederate states fought in the Battle of the Wilderness, while 18 of the 24 Union states drew their weapons. For the first time, General Robert E. Lee and General Grant met in combat. General Thomas Jonathan "Stonewall" Jackson, shot mistakenly by his own troops, lost his left arm. Beverley Tucker Lacy, J. Horace's brother and chaplain to the general, wrapped up Jackson's arm and laid it to rest in the family cemetery a few hundred yards from Ellwood. Contracting some type of infection, Jackson passed away six days later. This struck Robert E. Lee at his core.

Serving as a headquarters for both Confederate and Union troops, Ellwood's home and grounds functioned also as a field hospital for Confederate soldiers after the Battle of Chancellorsville. Some 26,000 men were either lost, wounded, captured, or died during the encounters. Many, especially the injured, perished in the rampant fire that broke out, engulfing soldiers who couldn't get away.

John Hennessy shares the following about Ellwood Manor's slave history:

The first known reference to William Jones's residence in "the Wilderness" comes not from a diary or travelogue, but from an advertisement for a runaway slave. "A remarkable likely, well made Mulatto man named DICK, about 27 years." Jones offered the substantial sum of five British pounds "if delivered to me at Wilderness, in Spotsylvania." William Jones's hunt for Dick hints at something essential about Ellwood: its enslaved residents.

Before the Civil War, Ellwood consisted of more than 3,000 acres of land. While most was leased or in timber, hundreds fell under the plow or hoe—hoes handled by the men

and women who would live out their lives (and whose children often lived out their lives) responding to the seasonal rhythms: sow, tend, harvest. By 1860, Ellwood was one of the most productive farms in the region—worth more than $30,000 and producing bushels of wheat and corn by the hundreds, all of it tended by enslaved people.

In 1860, just under 50 slaves worked the buildings, fields, and woods at Ellwood. They lived in 8 small houses scattered across the property. With the coming of war, owner J. Horace Lacy joined the Confederate army. At least two of his slaves ran away and joined the Union army. One, Andrew Weaver, was wounded in the Battle of Crater at Petersburg. Another, Charles Sprout, is one of just a few African-American soldiers buried in the National Cemetery in Fredericksburg.

We know little of the individual slaves who lived their lives at Ellwood, toiling in the service of owners William Jones and J. Horace Lacy. While we are drawn to the "big house" because of its elegance and setting (on a grassy knoll overlooking rolling farmland), and while we know not where the cabins of slaves stood or where their graves lie, in fact the slaves' place is all around: the fields, the forests, the forgotten corners of a plantation. Here life rolled in its relentless rhythm, and here slaves toiled against heat and bondage because they simply had no choice. That, as much as the sturdy bricks the house stands upon, is part of Ellwood's fabric and foundation.

The Lacys returned to Chatham in 1872, selling the plantation to pay off debts. Mrs. Lacy felt a sense of indescribable loss, as her childhood home was no more.

Ellwood was sold only once before passing to the National Park Service. Hugh Evander Willis-Jones took over the plantation's affairs in 1907, and he cared for the property until 1977. Two original slave quarters used to be present; however, the new family found them highly offensive and burned them down. Currently part of the Fredericksburg and Spotsylvania National Military Park's 2,774 acres, Ellwood is now a mere 183 acres. As the last standing structure from the Battle of Wilderness, the plantation home is cherished by its caretakers, who call themselves Friends of Wilderness Battlefield Incorporated (FOWB).

Aquia sandstone was used to build the exterior stairs. This is the same sandstone used for the White House, extracted from what used to be called Public Quarry and now referred to as

Government Island. Inside, black-painted floors conceal blood stains left from days gone by, when the building served as a hospital. Upstairs, four unfurnished rooms sit barely untouched. Hauntingly beautiful, a moment of reverence is expected as men, regardless of what side they fought on, lost their lives fighting for their beliefs. Great men such as Generals Grant and Lee militarily decided the fate of thousands, bearing the weight of a nation and conversely a coalition of states on their shoulders. The winner would undoubtedly be revered as a hero, the loser with the sympathies of his supporters. Only one piece in the home is known to have come from the Lacys, a lone silver fork.

Century-old pecan, black walnut, eastern red cedar, honey locust, Kentucky coffeetree, sugar maple, Osage orange, and American elm trees dot the grounds, which are abundantly lush with perennial plants. An herb garden peeks from out of the grass. But what's more impressive is that about 20 feet from the house is a depression where trees arch upwardly, slightly at an angle. The slump in the ground was made by an 18th-century carriage trail that no longer exists. The sound of horses drawing wooden wagons over battered terrain can almost be heard. And the volume must have been great, since the angled slope appears to be caving in on itself. To the unsuspecting eye, it's an area warped with time; to those who are aware, a lost memory.

Farther down the slope, open, cleared fields of corn no longer bear the tragedies of war. Timber is still plentiful, but a lone tree single-handedly guards the only tomb enclosed within a wooden fence. Yes, this is where Stonewall Jackson's arm is buried, enshrined for all to pay their respects. Returning to the house, the FOWB's next project is under way: the restoration of a 20th-century brooder barn which sits modestly behind the home. Almost nothing has changed in the 150 years since the War Between the States. Chatham still stands proudly across the Rappahannock. Mr. Jones and his descendants' legacy is retold on a daily basis, recounting their bravery, commitment, and willingness to go against the grain. The plantation continues to produce crops while those who are passionate about its future defend it tirelessly. This is Ellwood.

Gunston Hall

10709 Gunston Road
Mason Neck, VA 22079
(703) 550-9220
www.gunstonhall.org

JUST AROUND THE RIVER BEND

George Mason IV was born on Virginia soil on December 11, 1725. His father, George Mason III, catapulted the family into one of wealth as an American businessman and planter, while his mother, Ann Thomson Mason, was a member of the English aristocracy. Together George III and Ann's land holdings provided a comfortable life for their children.

The oldest of three siblings, George inherited a large tract of land after his father was killed in a ferry accident, 20,000-plus acres to be exact. For a man of 21, even by today's standards, that is a significant amount. By the time George turned 25, cupid's arrow struck him deeply as he began to court Ann Eilbeck, age 16. A business-minded man at all times, George also viewed Ann as an investment, since as an only child she was set to inherit all of her family's wealth.

After their marriage, George and Ann lived in another house that he owned in Dogue's Neck, Virginia, now known as Mason Neck, while the construction of Gunston Hall began around 1755. Built in the classic Georgian style, the home is composed of a Flemish bond; however, stonework also encases each corner of the house, showcasing a harmonious mix of the two materials.

At one point Mr. Mason wrote to his younger brother, Thomson, who was studying law in London, to send to America a skilled craftsman to complete the interior of the plantation home. Thomson complied, sending architect William Buckland to work as an indentured servant to complete the family's home. Buckland brought with him a flair for applying London's contemporary design and regarded the home as a blank canvas. Working closely with master carver William Bernard Sears, Buckland completed the home in 1759.

Quite statuesque, the stately home commanded one's attention with a panoramic view of the Potomac River. Guests who visited by boat entered through a Neo-Gothic portico on the river side

of the house. George Mason enjoyed amiably questioning guests about the number of Blackheart cherry trees planted in an allée leading to the land-side portico. The allée was positioned in such a way that when standing in the center of the porch, guests could only see the first tree in each row, but when they stepped slightly off center on either side, they could see the amassed number of 200 trees precisely placed.

The Masons owned about 100 slaves at Gunston Hall, divided by their skill craft. James, Mason's entrusted mulatto slave, along with a few select others, lived in Log Town on the western side of the plantation, separated by a row of trees that granted a bit of privacy from the ever-watchful master's eyes. Greeted by James at the front door, guests who arrived during Virginia's stifling summers sat in the main hallway where both doors were opened, allowing a cool breeze to flow in from the Potomac. The primary floor's four rooms are unique, as Buckland accentuated each room through the use of woodwork, color, and specific purpose.

As you enter the Chinese Room, painted bright yellow, English wallpaper made to replicate Chinese gardens decorates the walls. Facing the long drive, dinner guests could look out and see parts of the 5,500-acre tobacco farm in all its glory, but the point was to notice the chinoiserie-style carpentry along the walls that look like Chinese pagodas. Believed to have displayed fine pieces of china, dining companions were quickly made to understand the wealth of the Mason family. Afterward, perhaps the men retreated to the adjacent Palladian Room to smoke cigars and play cards while the women stayed behind and drank tea.

Named after Andrea Palladio, the famous Venetian architect, the Palladian Room is absolutely breathtaking. As you pass between original black walnut doors with an ornamental egg and dart border carved around the interior sections, the yellow pine floors creak beneath you. When your eyes finally adjust to the luxurious red-embroidered wallpaper, you're transported to a time when pomp and circumstance was considered the norm. The dark furniture includes some original pieces from the Mason family, while precious objects grace the beaufat cupboards that flank the fireplace.

The Little Parlor is plain compared to the other rooms, but the family usually sat here and enjoyed each other's company when the more formal Chinese Room wasn't being utilized. On the wall a Fry-Jefferson map of Virginia hangs, once considered one of the most accurate maps of its time. It was drawn by Joshua Fry and Peter Jefferson, both of whom were highly regarded as excellent land surveyors by their peers.

Across the hall, in stark contrast, is the Chamber, a bright green-hued room complete with a large canopy bed. It is here that Mrs. Mason gave birth to her 12 children, but only 9 survived. In 1773, at the age of 39, Ann died. John, the fourth surviving son, recalls in his memoirs that his mother loved to ride horses and kept her crop and riding clothes in the right closet of the room. Under lock and key, the opposite closet contained valuable ingredients and spices, bought perhaps from John Glassford & Company, a trading store at the mouth of the Occoquan River that sold luxury goods. After Ann died, George married Sarah Brent of Stafford County in 1780. Her father, George Brent, owned Woodstock Plantation on Aquia Creek. His cash crop was tobacco as well, a staple of Virginia's economy.

Exit the Chamber into the hallway, where a secret set of winding wooden stairs curves up to the second floor. Mostly used by house slaves attending to the children upstairs, the stairs aren't easy to navigate. With seven rooms in total, the second floor was heavily trafficked with the pitter-patter of the Mason children's feet. One can only imagine and sympathize with Mrs. Newman, the children's governess, and Mr. Constable, their teacher, whose hands were apparently full with the large brood.

On the homestead everything appeared fine, but a storm was brewing between the colonies and the English crown as dissidence continued to grow. Sympathetic to the colonies' grievances, Mason understood that they were currently at a critical point in time.

As treasurer of the Ohio Company and a member of the Fairfax County Committee of Safety and the Virginia Convention in Williamsburg, Mason was no stranger to political service. In May of 1776 he drafted the Virginia Declaration of Rights, a document unlike anything else in its time. Highlighting that "all Men are born equally free and independent," the final draft passed June 12. Less than two weeks later, Mason contributed heavily to the Virginia Constitution. With this document, the commonwealth broke from the Crown. It too was adopted by the Virginia Convention. The wording used in it both fueled the fire and was the basis of the Declaration of Independence. Although Mason did not sign the Declaration of Independence, he was a prominent member of the committee that designed the seal for the Commonwealth of Virginia shortly after.

The American Revolution as well as the Civil War took a toll on the house, passing through the hands of Edward Daniels (1868–1891) and Joseph Specht (1891–1907). In 1912, Louis Hertle bought and restored the property to its original grandeur with his second wife, Eleanor Daughaday. The house became a place of entertaining during the 1920s. Upon his death in 1949, Louis bequeathed Gunston Hall to the Commonwealth of Virginia, with the provision that it be managed by representatives of the National Society of Colonial Dames of America.

A museum chronicling Mason's life now stands just a few hundred yards from Gunston Hall. Looking out onto the Potomac River from the 250-year-old boxwood garden, your vantage point is almost exactly what George Mason, one of the Founding Fathers, saw every day: a new land with infinite possibilities.

Liberia Plantation

8601 Portner Avenue
Manassas, VA 20109
(703) 368-1873
www.manassasmuseum.org

THE BIRTHPLACE OF THE AMERICAN CIVIL WAR

Less than 6 miles from the first battle of the Civil War sits Liberia Plantation. Nestled in the woods, along a winding road, the house patiently waits for visitors to arrive. Often overshadowed by its more famous counterparts, the plantation holds a wealth of knowledge surrounding some of the most infamous battles in the deadliest war on American soil.

Liberia Plantation was built in 1825 by the great-great-granddaughter of Robert "King" Carter, Harriet Bladen Mitchell Weir, and her husband, William James Weir. The couple took extreme pride in constructing the Federal/Georgian-style home, lovingly called the "Brick House." Sitting on 2,000 acres considered part of the Lower Bull Run Tract at the beginning of the Civil War, the plantation included various other buildings such as a general store, the Liberia Academy, a post office, and family cemetery.

Flemish bond brickwork decorates the front side of the home, where each layer is composed of alternating stretchers (the exposed length of the brick) and headers (the exposed width of the brick). This technique signified the Weirs' wealth; however, the other sides of the home showcase an English bond, one of the oldest and most traditional types of masonry work during the 17th and 18th centuries.

The plantation prospered with the Weirs' investment in grain, vegetables, and livestock, and they owned one of the largest producing mills in Prince William County. Mr. Weir understood his position, as he was a member of one of the most powerful families in Virginia, and continued to solidify business deals until the Civil War. Selling a piece of his land to the Orange & Alexandria Railroad Company, he allowed the rail's extension northward toward Washington City.

As tensions grew over the issue of slavery, Virginia voted to remain pro-slavery and seceded from the Union soon after, on April 17, 1861. Confederate soldiers based in Alexandria left a month later, on May 24, and began heading farther south into the state. Union troops entered the Manassas area on July 21. After the first shots were fired, the gravity of the situation became clear, and Liberia Plantation stood in the crosshairs.

Confederate General P. G. T. Beauregard's officers set up headquarters within the home's 18-inch-thick walls. From there, orders were barked out to a ready and willing Confederate States of America (CSA) army. After the Confederates won the First Battle of Manassas, President Jefferson Davis

awarded the successful general a battlefield promotion. Realizing the danger in the area, the Weirs fled to Fluvanna County, leaving their beautiful home behind for slaves to keep safe.

Nonetheless, Liberia Plantation knew both sides in the war, as a year later General Irvin McDowell also made the home his headquarters in March of 1862. After McDowell was injured in a riding incident, his visitors included President Abraham Lincoln as well as Treasury Secretary Salmon Chase. It is said Chase and McDowell sat on the back porch, smoked cigars, and ate ice cream. Whether that occurred or not, the home is thought to be the only one in which both presidents visited their comrades during the Civil War. Walking up the exact same stairs and through the entryway, it is difficult not to wonder what secrets are held within the walls.

The two-story bricked home has unveiled a few of its secrets, but many are still being discovered. The original wood flooring provides an authentic touch to the current historic house museum. Walking into the dining room where Luisa Ball Weir entertained and fed her large family of seven children, you can sense the chaos experienced at dinner. Though the extension of the house is gone, you can see where a door once stood, leading out to the kitchen where slaves prepared the family's meals.

A registered member of the American Colonization Society (ACS), an organization that assisted with the emigration of freed slaves who wanted to return in Africa, William Weir aptly named his plantation Liberia. Conversely, with 80 enslaved people working on Liberia Plantation, the position of the Weirs is often called into question. Not much is known about slave life on the plantation, with the exception of one man by the name of Samuel Naylor. In November 1865 his wife Nelly, who stayed and cared for Liberia during the war years, was given 12½ acres of land by the Weir family in "consideration of the love and affection to their former servant." That land was in addition to the 65 acres that the Weirs sold to Samuel and Nelly for $525. Samuel had earlier purchased his freedom and saved enough to buy the land.

When the Weirs returned to Liberia Plantation after the war, time and neglect had wreaked havoc on the property, never to return to its prior glory. In 1888 the Weir family sold the plantation to Robert Portner, a German immigrant who became a powerful shipping merchant as well as owner of the Robert Portner Brewing Company in Alexandria, Virginia. Portner later turned the land surrounding Liberia into a profitable dairy farm, then sold the property to Hilda and Irving Jackson Breeden in 1947.

As Manassas continued to grow from an agricultural town into a city, the Breedens began selling the land around the plantation to developers in addition to developing apartment complexes and homes on their own. Donated by the couple to the City of Manassas in 1986 along with 5.6 acres of land, Liberia is now managed by the Manassas Museum System. Later the city purchased another 12.6 acres to serve as a shield from the rapid growth of the city.

In 2004 the museum began a much-needed restoration project. Peeling paint and water damage were just a couple of the issues faced, but today those problems no longer exist. Tours are held Sunday at noon during the summer, but other Basement to Attic tours and special events like Civil War Weekend are regularly scheduled throughout the year. A woman in period garb greets you at the door and takes you through the home, showing a family tree of the extensive reach of the Carter family as well as photographs of important visitors to the home during the Civil War.

Heading upstairs to the second floor, you'll discover names on the wall of Civil War soldiers who were either stationed in the area or just passing through, along with names of the Weir children marking their height or that of Captain Levin Bevin Day. It is said that Captain Day stood in the window the morning before the Second Battle of Manassas and looked out on the horizon before signing his name in a grandiose fashion. An upstairs room bears another similar display of penmanship and even an arithmetic problem that dates back to the 19th century. Behind the house sits the family cemetery where the Weirs and some of their children are buried behind a padlocked gate.

Before leaving Liberia Plantation, pause to realize that less than 6 miles away a critical battle sparked the Civil War.

3200 Mount Vernon Highway
Mount Vernon, VA 22121
(703) 780-2000
www.mountvernon.org

THE HOME OF AMERICA'S FIRST PRESIDENT

One of the most visited plantations in the United States, Mount Vernon is no ordinary mansion. George and Martha Washington once called the 11,028-square-foot estate home. Since being acquired by the Mount Vernon Ladies' Association in 1860, the property has expanded beyond its mansion, outbuildings, slave quarters, and farmland to include a restaurant as well as a world-renowned library and research center. The association's dedication to upholding George Washington's legacy has led to a collection of well-documented information ranging from what George ate for breakfast to his most private thoughts. Furthermore, Mount Vernon's records of its enslaved population provide details that shed light on a subject that is rarely discussed.

George Washington was a complex man, holding many titles such as president, general, planter, slave owner, experimental farmer, and entrepreneur, with Mount Vernon serving as the backdrop. Born February 22, 1732, to Augustine Washington and his second wife, Mary Ball, George was the oldest of six children. Augustine died in 1743, leaving the 11-year-old George a considerable amount of land and 10 slaves. Despite that inheritance, young Washington and his family found themselves in an unstable financial position, since resources had to be conserved to ensure the family's future. Unlike his older half-brothers Augustine and Lawrence, George was educated within the colony until he was a teenager. Assisting his mother with daily duties around his childhood plantation, Ferry Farm, located along the Rappahannock River, George began to learn and practice his lifelong interest in farming.

In 1735 George's father built Little Hunting Creek plantation, a one-and-a-half-story farmhouse. George's half-brother Captain Lawrence Washington (later promoted to a major) renamed the plantation after Admiral Edward Vernon, someone he looked up to. George, however, wouldn't

take over the plantation until 1754, leasing it from Lawrence's widow, Ann Fairfax, a member of the prominent Fairfax family, and her second husband, George Lee. When Ann died in 1761, Mount Vernon became his.

In 1758 George met Martha Dandridge Custis, the young widow of Daniel Parke Custis, a wealthy planter. Left with over 17,500 acres and almost 300 slaves after Daniel's death, Martha was an attractive catch to many bachelors, especially George, who had been introduced to Virginia's gentry by Lawrence. Without a will, a third of Daniel Custis's slaves—known as dower slaves—were given to Martha to use throughout her lifetime, but upon her death those slaves would be returned to Custis's heirs. After George and Martha married in 1759, he controlled her slaves but was not able to own them or change their enslaved status.

Washington the slave owner is less well known than Washington the lieutenant colonel during the French and Indian War and later general in the American Revolution. These positions would assist in defining his character as a fair, honest, and respected man among his peers and those who served under him. They would furthermore lay the groundwork for his path to the presidency.

Washington's first military encounter occurred in 1753 when he was 21 years old. Lieutenant Governor Dinwiddie of Virginia ordered him to deliver to French Captain Jacques Legardeur de Saint Pierre at Fort LeBoeuf a letter commanding the French to leave the area and stop pestering British traders. Traveling into Ohio territory, Washington returned with news that the French would not comply. That response led to the beginning of the French and Indian War. George fought for five long years before victory in 1758; however, his tenacity would prove to be instrumental to a later war that would birth a new nation.

Entering into politics in 1758, Washington served for 15 years in Virginia's House of Burgesses. During that time the relationship between Britain and the colonies continued to deteriorate, eventually leading to war. Appointed commander of the Continental army on June 15, 1775, Washington would go on to command his troops until 1781. His siege of Yorktown was a defining moment, proving the colonies' strength and determination for independence.

Washington stepped down from his position after victory, but his disappearance from the limelight was short-lived, as in 1789 he was elected the first president of the United States. He served for two consecutive terms from 1789 to 1797, assisting with key aspects of America's development, such as the creation of a federal currency as well as structuring of the Supreme Court. Having resided at executive mansions both in New York and Philadelphia during his terms, he and Martha returned to their beloved Mount Vernon after he left office.

Washington acquired more than 70 slaves by purchase and inheritance over the course of his life, in addition to the 10 his father willed him. He and Martha would have a total of more than 300 slaves upon his death in 1799. Most of the increase was due to birth of children in the slave community. In accordance to a Virginia law passed in December 1662, the status of children depended on that of their mother. From 1754 to 1773 Washington obtained other tracts of land surrounding Mount Vernon's original 2,126-acre plot, quadrupling his holdings.

George divided the plantation's enslaved population among five farms: the Mansion House, Dogue Run, Muddy Hole, River, and Union (previously called Ferry Farm). The Mansion House Farm differed from the others as it wasn't solely agricultural, but also included workshops and gardens. Many of those who worked in the mansion or at Mansion House Farm lived in the Greenhouse Slave Quarters adjacent to the manicured upper gardens. These quarters were built between 1791 and 1792 in a barracks-like style as extended wings added to the greenhouse that was completed in 1787. A bit more information on the 60 to 90 people who lived in these quarters is available than on many of the other enslaved people who worked at Mount Vernon.

Austin, one of Martha's dower slaves, was of mixed race and served as a waiter at Mount Vernon. He accompanied Martha to visit George during the Revolution, and also traveled to Philadelphia and New York when George was president and resided at both executive mansions. In 1780 a law had passed in Pennsylvania known as the Act for the Gradual Abolition of Slavery, stating that after six months of residency, a slave would become free. To prevent this from happening to their slaves, George and Martha sent them back to Mount Vernon before the end of those six months. Austin died on his way back to Mount Vernon while crossing a river close to Harford, Maryland.

Some slaves that fought for their freedom actually managed to escape but constantly lived in fear. The daughter of an English tailor and dower slave, Betty Oney "Ona" Judge was a seamstress and personal servant to Martha. After walking out while the Washingtons were having dinner in Philadelphia, Oney resisted numerous attempts by their aides to return her. Her fugitive status did not dissuade her from settling in Portsmouth, New Hampshire, in 1796.

In contrast, both Sambo Anderson and Hercules were not of mixed race but were highly regarded by George. Sambo was trained by master carpenter William Bernard Sears, who not only worked on Mount Vernon but also Gunston Hall, the home of George Mason IV, another affluent planter. Escaping in 1781 on the British warship *Savage*, he was later returned but was one of the slaves George freed in his will. After receiving his freedom, Sambo earned his living selling wild game.

Hercules's story was much different. Celebrated for his exceptional skills as a chef, he accompanied the newly appointed commander in chief to Pennsylvania in 1790. Yet like many of those who traveled to work at the executive mansion, Hercules was sent back before he could claim residency. Upon arriving back in Virginia and perhaps due to Washington's soon-to-be retirement in 1797, Hercules's culinary skills were not needed for a few months. He and other house servants were sent outside to work in the gardens or with the bricklayers. Seeing this as an insult, Hercules ran away to seek his freedom in 1797. As with Oney, George pursued Hercules but with no success. It is thought that the portrait of Hercules as a chef, painted by the acclaimed artist Gilbert Stuart, is one of the few depictions of an enslaved person during the 18th century.

Those slaves who worked on Washington's other four farms were supervised at all times by an overseer who might have been hired or enslaved himself. William Garner and William Stewart both oversaw River Farm (1788–1792 and 1794–1797 respectively), Joseph Cash worked at Dogue Run Farm (1796–1797), John Violet at Union Farm (1796–1797), and John Fairfax at Mansion House Farm (1784–1790). These men, among others, kept a watchful eye over the plantation. One of Washington's longtime employees was Jonathan Alton, who worked for 30 years as an overseer, from 1755 to 1785. Other men like Turner Crump and Thomas Brooks oversaw skilled enslaved laborers such as carpenters. These overseers were paid with wages, food, and other products throughout their tenure at Mount Vernon.

Conversely, master farmer and estate manager Anthony Whiting (1790–1793) or William Pearce (1793–1796) would report to Washington on the plantation's operational production and the daily activities of both slaves and overseers on a weekly basis, even while he traveled. With a roof over their heads while working for one of the most respected men in America, these men kept Mount Vernon running smoothly.

Accounts of how George Washington treated his slaves vary. He wanted his plantation to run efficiently for optimal profit and was known to threaten and use his power to control his slaves. Yet one thing is clear: Over the course of his lifetime, Washington's views on slavery changed from being a fact of life to wanting to wash his hands of it completely. Interactions with individuals such as Phyllis Wheatley, an educated slave who became a known published poet, and the Marquis de Lafayette, who strongly opposed slavery, led Washington to realize the hypocrisy of the new country whose ideology stood on the principles of freedom and equality for all people. Unlike his counterparts, Washington was the only major Founding Father to free all of his slaves in his will. He died on December 14, 1799, and noted that his slaves should be freed upon Martha's death.

Friends who knew of his request convinced Martha to release the slaves early for fear she would be killed to expedite the process. A little over a year later, Martha freed her husband's slaves; nonetheless, January 1, 1801, may have been one of the happiest and saddest days for those 123 slaves. Many of them had married and started families with Martha's dower slaves, who would be returned to the Custis estate upon her death. Martha Washington died on May 22, 1802.

Washington had begun to enlarge the farmhouse at Mount Vernon in 1758, raising its roof to add an additional story. But 1774 saw the largest growth, as the north and south wings were begun as well as the mansion's rooftop cupola. The cupola served as a ventilation system, pulling in the warm and humid air circulating through the house and pushing it out when its windows were open. It also gave a panoramic view of the surrounding landscape. Guests would typically enter the carriage side known as the West Front. Overlooking a 12-acre bowling green, Mount Vernon was expanded to a 21-room mansion with fruit orchards, well-kept gardens, stables, a botanical garden that served as a nursery for rare plants, and outbuildings such as a distillery and a gristmill.

The plantation's beauty is undeniable, with its red-painted cypress roof contrasting sharply against its white woodwork. On the first floor, Mount Vernon, like many Virginia plantations of that time, had a grand central passage. Take a peek at the Key of the Bastille, a gift given to Washington by his friend the Marquis de Lafayette, hanging on the wall. Dating to 1735, the small dining room is part of Augustine Washington's original farmhouse and reflects his wealth in the technique used to obtain the luminous green color of its walls. The paint contained a copper pigment, and when copper corrodes, a chemical reaction causes a green residue to be left behind. The room would require constant maintenance, as over time the copper in the walls' paint would oxidize, turning black. Its ornate mantel was carved by master carpenter William Bernard Sears.

Walking from the dining room into Washington's study, you can see items George held dear. A chain used to survey land commemorates his time as a surveyor as an adolescent. The iron chest holding part of Washington's wealth was kept under lock and key. His secretary bookcase showcases expert craftsmanship of the time period. It is easy to envision the 6-foot, 2-inch Washington sitting at his desk writing in his diary or composing one of the numerous letters he would write to friends and colleagues. George and Martha would correspond frequently during his time in the Continental army. Unfortunately, only two of those letters survived, found behind the drawer of a desk, as Martha destroyed their entire correspondence before her death.

In the Little Parlor, four artworks by Martha's youngest granddaughter, Eleanor "Nelly" Parke Custis, hang proudly. A talented artist, Nelly's watercolors and drawings illustrated her proficiency in the skill, as women of her class were expected to demonstrate adeptness in music, the arts, and languages. In the adjoining New Room, a gorgeous 14-foot Palladian window looks out to the bowling green. Here some of the Washingtons' guests were dined and entertained. As the largest room in Mount Vernon, George displayed his wealth through its artworks and furnishings, including the Federal-style sideboard by Philadelphian cabinetmaker John Aitken. A marble mantel is just as decorative, depicting the rural life of a general who returned to farming after saving his country. From the New Room, original yellow pine floors lead into a room brilliantly painted a gorgeous shade of Prussian blue. The West Parlor represented the Washingtons with family portraits. It also served as a social setting for their most cherished friends.

The second floor gives way to four magnificent bedchambers. Immediately to the left of the stairwell is the Blue Room. As Washington continued to expand Mount Vernon, he was able to divide the space into two: one being the Blue Room, the other called the Lafayette Room, paying homage to his dear friend the Marquis de Lafayette. Washington was quite fond of Lafayette, giving him a bedchamber that could only be upstaged by his own. Decorated in a floral-style "chintz" pattern, emulating expensive textiles from India, it looks out onto the Potomac River. It is believed General Lafayette stayed here during his travels, which is why you'll see a portrait of him hanging in the room. The Small Room, previously known as the Hall Room, lost much of its square footage when the third level was added. Though not as large as the other bedchambers, it does have its own window.

Eleanor "Nelly" Custis's bedroom is also on this floor. This was the room where Nelly gave birth to her first child, Frances Parke Lewis. She was the only child of Eleanor's that George met and blessed before his death. This room also holds her crib as well as a warming pan, a tool that would hold hot coals and when placed between the sheets for a few moments would provide warmth on frigid winter nights. The Yellow Room displays a part of the bell system, more of which can be seen outside on the east-facing piazza, and leads to the Washingtons' bedchamber. Inside the couple's classically decorated room, the bed George died in still remains. From a French writing desk belonging to Martha to portraits of their adored grandchildren, the room provides a glimpse into the private lives of America's first presidential couple.

In the garret, or third floor, smaller rooms were used by the family for sleeping and storage. Entertaining over 677 visitors in one year alone, the Washingtons were popular, to say the least. One of the rooms has a stove designed by none other than Benjamin Franklin that provided a better source of heat than previous fireplaces. Martha chose to stay in this room after the death of her husband, which had affected her greatly. This is also the level providing access to the 360-degree cupola.

Down in the cellar, numerous rooms housed various products including Madeira and dry goods, while the cellar kitchen was where servants were expected to take their meals. From the cellar you can access the West Front or East Front and its piazza that faces out toward the river.

Mount Vernon has outbuildings in abundance. The 16-sided barn is a marvelous design, thought of by Washington himself, allowing wheat berries to fall between symmetrically spaced floorboards down into a granary. Closer to the mansion, the north lane leads to the blacksmith shop where skilled laborers toiled. The overseer and mansion slave quarters are located on this side as well. There is access to the botanical gardens where Washington would test new plants before planting them on his large estate, in addition to his upper garden, which served as a pleasure garden. However, it still had a functional purpose, as perennials and such would surround his smaller vegetable plots.

The lower garden produced strawberries, grapes, cabbage, and peas, to name a few. Opening up to the nursery and fruit garden, George planted apples, pears, and peaches. Here it is easy to access the animal pens and south lane leading to the stables where Washington's revered war horses were kept.

The new tomb holds the bodies of 22 Washington family members as well as two marble sarcophagi containing the bodies of Martha and George. Whether you walk to the Potomac Wharf where Washington operated his fisheries, the cemetery and memorial honoring the Washingtons' slaves, the four-story gristmill where grains were ground into meal or flour, or the two-story distillery, there is much to be seen. After a full day of exploring, you may be a bit famished. Make sure to stop by the Mount Vernon Inn Restaurant. Tasty dishes like the Colonial hoecake topped with country ham, sautéed crabmeat with hollandaise, or Virginia peanut soup are readily available, but reservations are highly recommended.

Much can be said for the first president of the United States, his wife Martha, and their precious grandchildren. Their history has been preserved due to the labor of love and wisdom of the Mount Vernon Ladies' Association of the Union, founded in 1853 by Ann Pamela Cunningham. Seeing the disrepair Mount Vernon had fallen into, she petitioned John Augustine Washington III to sell the property. Miss Cunningham and the ladies raised the $200,000 necessary to purchase the mansion and 200 acres. Today the association, along with the loving support of donors, continues to keep Washington's memory and legacy alive.

Sully Historic Site

3650 Historic Sully Way
Chantilly, VA 20151
(703) 437-1794
www.fairfaxcounty.gov/parks/sully-historic-site

ALMOST LOST TO AVIATION

Tucked quietly away along Route 28 in Fairfax County is Sully Historic Site. Airplane engines rumble while cars pass by in the distance. It wasn't always like this, as the 130-acre property currently partially owned by both the Federal Aviation Association and Fairfax County Park Authority used to be much larger, roughly 3,000 acres. However, as the area circling the District of Columbia became populous, so did interest in its development, including the acreage surrounding Sully.

Dulles International Airport (IAD), commissioned in 1958 by President Dwight Eisenhower, opened its doors to the public in 1962. Originally slated to grow to 10,000 acres over the next 50-odd years, Dulles has reached that goal plus 2,000 acres more with its latest land acquisition in 2004. The area is expansive, handling numerous international airlines such as Air Lingus, AeroMexico, and Emirates, to name a few. Perhaps not as utilized as its counterparts in Baltimore, Maryland (BWI), and Arlington, Virginia (DCA), Dulles is the largest of the trio in land mass, making it one of the fastest-expanding airports in the United States, which contributed to Sully's survival. Neighboring buffer zones surrounding Dulles lie less than 4 miles from Sully's borderline, but the site prevails against the challenges of an ever-expanding area. Thanks to the efforts of Frederick Nolting, the property's last private owner; Edward "Eddie" Wagstaff, considered the site's first curator; and Eleanor Lee Templeman, a historian and Lee descendant, a bill passed by Congress prevented the FAA from demolishing the historic buildings.

A planter, as were most men of the Lee family, Richard Bland Lee's grandfather Henry Lee I acquired a land grant of over 3,000 acres in 1725 and began to cultivate tobacco. This continued with his son, Henry Lee II, until it passed onto Richard Bland Lee, third generation when wheat and corn became the main crops. Brother of Henry "Light Horse Harry" Lee, Richard was born January 20,

1761, and started building what is now known as Sully Historic Site in 1794 on the roughly 1,500 acres willed to him. Serving in the Virginia House of Delegates three times, he became Northern Virginia's first representative in the United States House of Representatives, an honor in itself.

Considered a Son of the American Revolution (SAR), a patriotic society composed of men whose male descendants fought in the Revolutionary War, Richard Lee was awarded a commissioner's position from James Madison to assess damage from the War of 1812 and remained a political supporter of the president; his wife, Elizabeth Collin Lee, and Dolley Madison were close friends, writing a series of letters to one another over the course of their lifetime. The Lees had nine children, four of whom lived into adulthood. Sully remained in their possession until 1811, when it was sold to Lee's cousin, Francis Lightfoot Lee II. By 1838 Sully left the last of Lee ownership when it was purchased by William Swartwort after years of disrepair.

During his time in Philadelphia, where Congress met in the late 18th century, Richard Lee took notice of the upper Mid-Atlantic's architecture, bringing that design back to Sully. Built at the turn of the 19th century, Sully mixes Georgian and Federal architecture while showcasing both Tidewater Virginia and Philadelphian influences. The main house was built in two stages. The first half, built throughout 1794, was two and a half stories aboveground. The second half was completed in 1799 with the east wing addition, one and a half stories high; both halves also incorporate full cellars. Unlike most plantation homes of the previous period, its configuration differed from Colonial Georgian symmetry. Yet it appears Mr. Lee spared no expense on interior or exterior decorations. For further insight, the Virginia Historical Society has two sets of plantation records, one from 1771 to 1865 and one from 1794 to 1836, though the latter is more on the family's affairs than those of Richard Bland Lee. A 2-acre garden stretched west of the home.

Dependencies, or "offices," including a kitchen, smokehouse, and dairy, were built outside of the home. Almost 20 feet long, the dairy's stonework is quite ornate. Its two-room second story was used as an apartment for a family, possibly early on. The smokehouse, 12 feet square, held salted and smoked meats and stood between the kitchen-laundry and the dairy. A covered walkway connected the main house to its kitchen-laundry, which by the 1900s housed African-American renter Jeff Harris and his family.

From the beginning of its existence until 1839, Sully was supported by slave labor. Accounts state that Richard Lee inherited 29 slaves from his father in 1787. A rarity, Sully has a well-documented

history of its enslaved population. Old Eave, one of the earliest slaves recorded (1746), and Madam Juba, a laundress, are just two life stories that are emphasized on the Forgotten Road Tour. Even runaway ads are well documented, specifically for Godfrey and Ludwell. Unfortunately, Ludwell was returned to Sully after his escape attempt. A reconstructed slave cabin is perched along the old south road, based on the archeological footprint. A few feet away are a cluster of structures with an average size of 16 by 20 feet.

In 2004 Sully's site manager, Carol McDonnell, assisted in the production of the award-winning video titled *From the Ground Up: The Sully Slave Quarter*, chronicling its 10-month construction, step by step. One of the few plantations that not only acknowledge but delve deeply into their enslaved past, Sully's Forgotten Road Tour raises important questions that may not usually be asked. Regardless of one's position, who these people were, including their names, occupations, and even tenures at Sully, is extremely important. As recently reported by the *Washington Post*, the Fairfax Circuit Court Historic Records Center now provides access to slave records through the Fairfax County Slave Index. Although not digitized, being able to research records that date back over a century is quite astounding. Furthermore, with thousands of entries available, it is one of the most comprehensive collections in Northern Virginia.

Slaves continued to work Sully until the 19th century, when Quakers began to move into Virginia as dairy production grew due to depletion of the soil by tobacco. When Jacob and Amy Haight, Quakers from New York, bought Sully in 1842 from William Swartwort, they forged a new path for the farm's future by utilizing modern agricultural practices like using different fertilizers. Suspected to be Union sympathizers, Jacob and his son, Alexander, both fled to Alexandria, leaving behind Amy and their married daughter, Maria Haight Barlow, to defend Sully. Both Union and Confederate troops stopped at the plantation, whether for food, medical attention, or simply to rest until the next set of orders arrived. Amy and Jacob died during the Civil War but had already left Sully's affairs to Maria and her husband, James. The home remained with the Barlows until 1869, when it was sold, and had seven more owners before the Fairfax County Park Authority took over in 1959.

Through research, the park authority discovered fun facts about the house and the families who previously lived there. One was the pet of the Lees. Dogs, cats, gerbils, or fish may come to mind when the family pet is discussed; however, the Lees owned a white squirrel, seen sitting atop the Lee's family crest. Mrs. Lee in 1810 describes "one of our greatest cares and amusements is the

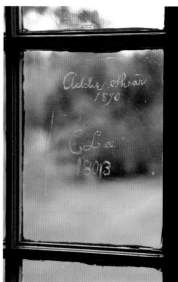

white squirrel who is now white indeed and beautiful. Mr. Lee this moment followed him all over the house—fearing he might again feel his natural propensity to escape, as it is the first time since our return he has been from his box . . ."

In 1969 Eddie Wagstaff left an endowment that started the Sully Foundation, Ltd., which has developed and funded various projects. At one point in time, a west wing was added to the home; however, it is now gone, as damage superseded restoration. But other projects were granted the green light, hiring artisans to assist with false graining on the beautiful doors or, in the 1980s, restoring floorboards in the entry hall to their unfinished look. Presently Sully Historic Site is undergoing a historic structure report that will set the tone for future projects completed by the team. Dropping by the kitchen-laundry is a must, as the two-room building is structurally sound. Additionally, ask to be escorted to the second floor of the building, where original beams are still visible.

You may see Sully from the air as you fly out of Dulles, or perhaps spy its beckoning road sign as you are speeding down Route 28. Before taking the tour, sit in one of the comfortable rocking chairs on the porch, gaze out onto the densely tree-lined horizon, and imagine the changes this home has experienced. Uniqueness was and still is one of Sully's best characteristics, and if its foundation has anything to do with the site's future, which we're sure it will, the improvement of what you currently see will continue to blossom.

Woodlawn Plantation

9000 Richmond Highway
Alexandria, VA 22309
(703) 780-4000
www.woodlawnpopeleighey.org

FOUR MILES FROM THE MOUNT VERNON ESTATE

The juxtaposition of two houses—one considered an architectural masterpiece, the other a historic part of the Washington-Lee family—sets the tone for visual stimulation. Four miles from George Washington's Mount Vernon Estate is Woodlawn. Built in 1805, it is almost 150 years older than Frank Lloyd Wright's Pope-Leighey House just a few feet away. Considered one of the greatest American architectural contributions of the 20th century, the Pope-Leighey House with its clean lines and utilitarian purpose does not take away from its Federal neighbor. Woodlawn was a part of George Washington's massive estate, though many people are unfamiliar with its history.

As George continued to win the hearts of the American people, Martha's two grandchildren came to live with the beloved couple. Upon reaching adulthood, Eleanor "Nelly" Parke Custis, the older of the two, married George's nephew, Lawrence Lewis, on Washington's last birthday, February 22, 1799. For a wedding gift, the couple was bestowed a 2,000-plus-acre farm along with the finances needed to build the home. Dr. William Thornton, American architect and mastermind behind the US Capitol, was commissioned to construct the newlyweds' abode. Somewhere between 1801 and 1805, construction began; however, ownership of Woodlawn only remained with the couple until 1846. Yet during those 40 years or so, its beauty reflected the epitome of a river-view Southern plantation.

From its grassy hills, Woodlawn's vantage point includes the Potomac River as well as Mount Vernon. An original horse chestnut tree slightly blocks a panoramic view from the perched portico. On the north side, the visitors' parking lot sits exactly where bricks were kilned over 200 years ago. A striking example of Flemish bond brickwork, the main house is connected to outer wings by attached, abridged hyphens. Those hyphens, referred to as "north" and "south," had different purposes within the home.

Each hyphen is drastically different from the rest of the house. Dirt floors and unfinished walls were enclosed behind a polished exterior; however, this is where servants and slaves came to receive their orders for the day, and it was a resting place between chores. The south hyphen is the more notable of the two, as it had an inside well where fresh water was drawn daily. This innovation was very uncommon but illustrated Woodlawn's modernization. Today part of the well is still located out of sight to the public within the basement.

Woodlawn is one of the best examples of Federal-style architecture in Northern Virginia. Flourishing from the late 17th to early 18th century, the Federal style is an American interpretation of ancient Roman architecture, differentiating from its gaudy Georgian predecessor with clean lines and a delicate simplicity. Woodlawn's main building, sans the hyphens and wings, illustrates this configuration.

A few significant points to look for are a two-storied rectangular building; a symmetrical line of windows, usually grouped in fives; and curved decorative stairwells. Moreover, roofline balustrades grace the large portico facing the river. With raised 14½-foot ceilings in the parlor room, sounds of musical notes from a harp, harpsichord, English guitar, piano forte, or violin could often be heard, as both Lawrence and Eleanor were proficient in classical instruments. Yet it is the floating staircase that commands the most attention before ascending to the second floor. Structured in a perfect oval, Dr. Thornton's engineering feat is a marvel of Federal architecture. Also notable are the wooden carvings on the bedposts. On one particular post various fruits, grains, and crops are expertly carved into what looks like black walnut. The pineapple engraving, symbolizing agriculture and fertility, is quite spectacular.

The exact number of slaves at Woodlawn is not available, but it is thought that Eleanor received up to 30 slaves upon her dowry. Wealth, as with many landowners, was displayed through proprietorship of property. Woodlawn's slave quarters no longer exist, but it is known that all aspects of plantation life were handled by the Lewises' slave population.

Prominent guests, such as the Marquis de Lafayette, popped in for long visits due to the arduous travel of that time period. Out of the eight children born, only three survived to adulthood. Mrs. Lewis's younger brother, George Washington Parke Custis, grew up to build Arlington House, also known as the Custis-Lee Mansion. The couple's son, Lorenzo, acquired Woodlawn after the death of his father in 1839. Tobacco had completely depleted the soil's nutrients, so a decision was made to sell the farm. Six years later, Lorenzo finally found a buyer in two Quaker families from New Jersey.

Those two families were the Troths and Gillinghams, who later went on to form the Troth-Gillingham Company, supplying prominent shipbuilder Joseph Gillingham. Rows and rows of trees grew, making their timber sourcing a very lucrative venture. As Quakers and staunch abolitionists, slavery was not supported. Additionally dividing their farmland into 200 smaller plots, the company paid wages to their workers, including blacks. Troth and Gillingham were able to establish a Free Labor Colony on the grounds of a former plantation, something regarded as a phenomenon since this was pre–Civil War. By the 1860s the number of enslaved African people was almost a third of Virginia's total demographic.

In 1850 the house was sold to the Masons, a Baptist family that had similar ideologies but did no major restoration to the house. Woodlawn was bought by a land development company in 1890 and left vacant for 11 years. In 1896 a hurricane slammed Southern Virginia and blew through Washington, DC, severely damaging the property. It wasn't until 1901 that Paul Kester, an American playwright, purchased the property and began to restore the home. Considered eclectic for his time, Kester moved to Europe but returned upon hearing that Gunston Hall, home of George Mason,

was in a state of disrepair. He also restored that home to its present glory. By 1905 Kester sold Woodlawn to Elizabeth Sharpe, a Pennsylvanian coal-mining heiress. Elizabeth continued revamping Woodlawn until her death in the early 1920s. In 1925 Alabamian politician Oscar Underwood bought the house, as his political career was moving in the direction of presidential candidate and with Woodlawn's close proximity to DC, it was a perfect match. However, he never received his party's nomination for the US presidency, mainly due to his vocal disapproval of the Ku Klux Klan.

After Underwood's death in 1929, his wife Bertha kept up the property until 1948, when she passed away. The Woodlawn Public Foundation took over its care and leased the property to the National Trust for Historic Preservation until 1957, when the trust purchased it outright and began to tackle several renovation projects. For the last 45 years, Woodlawn Plantation has seen its surrounding area change drastically, with the expansion of Richmond Highway / Route 1 / Jefferson Davis Highway.

Restoration and preservation have been extremely important to those who care for the site. One of the largest projects to date has been to repair the home's 86 windows. With windows ranging from the home's origins in 1805 to the 20th century, each one needed various amounts of attention. Beginning in 2012, the Cyprus windows were restored one by one; also added were louvered shutters and a UV ray coating. In a new innovative partnership, the Arcadia Center for Sustainable Food and Agriculture currently bases its farming operations on a portion of Woodlawn's property. This partnership allows Arcadia to run distinct food programs including a Farm to School Program, where students visit the farm; a training program for those involved in preparing healthier school meals; and the Veteran Farmer Program, which gives veterans the chance to be involved in a 12-month course learning how to farm.

One of Woodlawn's most visible events is its annual Needlework Exhibition, and the house is supported in part by Nelly's Needlers, established in 1975, who help run the show. Named after the first woman of the house, the group has raised almost $650,000 to benefit Woodlawn so far. Strictly composed of volunteers, a minimum of 50 hours is required to become involved. The needlework exhibition is held each March and draws attendees from near and far, with some of the youngest participants under 9 years old, the same age Nelly was when she begin to perform needlework.

Over 200 years, Woodlawn's ownership has changed hands six times, each owner being completely different from the one before; however, their common motivation was the knowledge that the site could make a difference in the community, and the utmost care and attention were given to the property. That focus has paid off. Woodlawn and Pope-Leighey House continue to remain significant in the 21st century, operating the buildings and grounds and creating the programs and partnerships that make a difference for those who still believe in the importance and benefits of local agriculture.

Virginia Mountains

Bordering West Virginia at the tip of Appalachian country, the end of one mountain range begins as another ends. Virginia's mountain region is a paradise for the outdoors enthusiast. One area is known as "Virginia's Switzerland," thanks to its alpine climate. Another boasts a section of the Appalachian Trail and was featured in the film *A Walk in the Woods* starring Robert Redford. There's a natural hot springs, now known as Jefferson Pools because of the third president who once sought healing in its waters. Poplar Forest, Jefferson's personal retreat and now a National Historic Landmark, is included in this chapter. Virginia's oldest covered bridge and the last remaining hump-back bridge in the United States is located here. The region's largest city is Roanoke, a shopping and dining destination.

Historic Avenel

413 Avenel Avenue
Bedford, VA 24523
(540) 586-1814
www.historicavenel.com

FOOTHILLS OF THE BLUE RIDGE HIGHLANDS

Perhaps best known as the birthplace of country music, the Blue Ridge Highlands sit at the base of the Blue Ridge Mountains. A part of the Appalachian Mountains, the Blue Ridge extends from Pennsylvania down to Georgia. Its rugged terrain creates a breathtaking landscape of rolling hills, lush meadows, and mountains which produce a nice amount of snow during the winter months. In the far southwestern part of Virginia lies the quaint town of Bedford, with a population of less than 10,000 people. The area's undisturbed terrain provides an unspoiled picture of what settlers may have seen upon their westward expansion in the early 19th century.

Avenel looks out onto a mid-19th-century neighborhood that didn't exist until after the Civil War. Once a thriving 200-acre plantation, Historic Avenel's ownership stayed within the realm of two families: the Burwells and the Ballards. In 1838 William M. Burwell and his wife, Frances Steptoe, had the blended Federal and Greek Revival–style mansion built. The floor plan was designed in a split-residence manner, which possibly stemmed from the extended Burwell family moving in upon completion of the home. William's widowed mother-in-law, Mrs. James C. Steptoe, along with her son Edward also lived with the couple.

When touring, pay attention to split-level stairs, each set leading to a separate part of the house. A peculiar second-floor interior window in the middle of the house perpetuates Avenel's unique design. Furthermore, the basement can only be accessed from an exterior entrance, with no inside connection between it and the mansion's interior. It could have served as Edward's separate quarters, with the division in the home for Mrs. Steptoe.

With four daughters in the family, Avenel was a busy place. Mr. Burwell was the son of William A. Burwell, a congressman from Franklin County and a secretary to Thomas Jefferson, and he

attempted to follow in his father's footsteps. While he pursued his political career, traveling often from Washington, DC, to New Orleans, Mrs. Burwell oversaw the home's daily chores and workers.

One of their daughters, Letitia M. Burwell, wrote a book titled *A Girl's Life in Virginia Before the War.* Her recounting of their life before the Civil War depicts one of happiness and contentment for everyone, including the slaves. She stated that she and her sisters taught some of the slaves to read (without consequence) and cared for those who were in need. Portraying slaves living a life of sheer delight, although readable (and imaginably true), the book is entirely one-sided. An account from the dominant, ruling class may or may not be considered biased due to one's position. Additionally, a dedication that reads "to my nieces, who will find in English and American publications such expressions applies to their ancestors as: 'cruel slave-owner'; 'inhuman wretches'; 'southern taskmasters'; 'dealers in human souls,' etc.," though heroic, appears to be an attempt to change others' opinions of the past. Regardless, one of their slaves, named Lucinda, was given the Burwells' surname and is buried in the family's plot

During the Civil War, General Robert E. Lee, along with his wife and other Lee family members, visited Avenel. The room dedicated to the general is nobly but simplistically decorated. It's located on Avenel's second floor in the southeast corner. Light fills the room, and a cream-colored settee contrasts against the dark wood and crimson curtains. The plantation did witness parts of the War Between the States, with Hunter's Raid happening in nearby Lynchburg in 1864. And before other homes were built around Avenel, tracks in the ground from passing carriages could still be seen.

Letitia lived at Avenel her entire life, until 1905. A year later, J. W. Ballard and family bought the property but did not operate it as a plantation. It remained in the Ballard family until 1985 when its last descendant, Peggy Ballard Maupin, left, moving to an apartment on the street behind Avenel. Interviewed on the television show *Sightings*, she speaks about the "Lady in White" who haunts the plantation and its grounds.

The Avenel Foundation bought the house in 1985. Overgrown with weeds and appearing quite haunted from its outside appearance, the foundation took its time restoring Avenel to its previous glory. The foundation's attention to detail is visible, as most of the plasterwork, moldings, and floors are original to the mansion. Paintings and photographs of the Burwells and the Ballards can be found inside the home, honoring both families' 150-year tenure of Historic Avenel.

Poplar Forest

1542 Bateman Bridge Road
Forest, VA 24551
(434) 525-1806
www.poplarforest.org

JEFFERSON'S PRIVATE OASIS

Originally more than 10 tulip poplars guarded Thomas Jefferson's private oasis; today there are only seven. Located on Virginia's frontier, Poplar Forest served as his personal retreat from his larger and more accessible mansion, Monticello. Yet it didn't become his full-fledged refuge until late in his second term as president. For most of his 50-plus years of ownership of the property, it functioned as a tobacco plantation, with its sole occupants being overseers and the enslaved people who toiled its fertile soil.

Thomas Jefferson was born on April 13, 1743, at Shadwell Plantation, 3 miles east of his beloved Monticello. His father, Peter Jefferson, worked as a land surveyor and was influential in young Tom's upbringing. Demanding that his son be properly educated, a common expectation among the gentry, Thomas was sent to boarding school when he was 8 years old. Studious, he learned the classics, and in 1760 entered the College of William & Mary. While there he met George Wythe, developing a student-teacher mentorship as well as an adopted son-father relationship. His determination and dedication to his studies paid off, and he graduated within two years.

By 1772 Thomas was no longer a child, and he fell in love with Martha Wayles Skelton on New Year's Day. Her father, John Wayles, was a wealthy planter and lawyer, and upon his death she inherited his 4,800-acre plantation, which then passed to Jefferson. In 1782, after 10 years of marriage, Martha died. Perhaps split between loyalty and sadness, and to honor the pledge that he made to his late wife, Jefferson would never remarry.

Jefferson's involvement in politics began in 1768 when he was elected to serve as a delegate in the House of Burgesses and then in 1775, the Continental Congress. A year later, at the age of 33, he wrote the Declaration of Independence. His mentor, George Wythe, also signed the famous

document. As the Revolutionary War raged on, Jefferson stayed at Poplar Forest for six months while British troops looked for him at Monticello and around the Charlottesville area.

Once the war ended, Jefferson served as minister to France for five years. During this time, he developed a love of French cooking. He returned to America as the French Revolution was beginning and soon achieved something no one had before, serving as the first secretary of state under President George Washington in 1790. He was then elected vice president under President John Adams in 1796, and four years later, in 1801, Thomas Jefferson became the third president of the United States.

Between 1805 and 1806 Jefferson ordered the firing of 250,000 bricks at Poplar Forest to construct his private retreat. Work on the house was done by John Hemings, a brother of Sally Hemings, who was the slave that Jefferson bore children with. John apprenticed with a master carpenter, and Jefferson expected him to use those skills to finish the interior work at Poplar Forest.

Like the other Founding Fathers, Jefferson was a celebrity during his lifetime, but he soon grew tired of the constant attention. Visitors, whether welcomed or not, would drop by the White House as well as Monticello unannounced, vying to meet the president. From 1801 to 1809 Jefferson lived at the White House and Monticello, and it wasn't until 1809 that he first stayed at his new personal retreat house at Poplar Forest.

Jefferson was one of America's first great architects. His design for Poplar Forest was influenced by the Italian architect Andrea Palladio and 18th-century French and English architecture. Poplar Forest was built in an octagonal shape for two reasons. First, Jefferson was an avid reader, and at any time had more than 1,000 books in his library. Without electricity, he certainly appreciated the light that the large windows allowed to enter the house. Second, Virginia's summers were hot and humid. With windows strategically located, the unusual shape provided for natural air-conditioning for Jefferson and his guests. In the front and back of the house, pay attention to the circular columns made up of semicircular brick. Also ingenious is the squint brick giving Poplar Forest its octagonal shape.

As he did at his Monticello home, Jefferson slept in an alcove bed at Poplar Forest. In the dining room, a dumbwaiter (a wooden shelving unit) at the corner of the table was used to serve his dinner. Take a peek at the Ridgeway pearlware that his food was served on. Realizing that additional space was needed, in 1814 Jefferson built an addition to the house that he called the Wing of Offices. The addition had four rooms that were used as storage space, a laundry, a kitchen, and a smokehouse.

Thomas Jefferson was a slave owner, inheriting 90 from his father and 135 from his father-in-law. Over the course of his life, he would own over 600 enslaved people, with about 90 residing at Poplar Forest. Known as chattel slavery, the practice where a person was considered property and therefore unable to own property themselves, it was a never-ending cycle.

From 1773 to 1809 overseers managed the plantation. All activity revolved around the tobacco fields, upon which Poplar Forest's livelihood depended. Cooks would strategically be placed in the fields, preparing food so that slaves could eat and get back to work quickly. A wagon would travel back and forth along the fields with a sharpener so that tools could either be replaced or sharpened on-site. Working from sunup to sundown, enslaved people provided the labor that made Jefferson's plantation work, which provided the lifestyle that he enjoyed.

Some slaves didn't accept their fate, and one such person was named Billy. He became enraged when he was asked to work on a Sunday, the only day slaves were allowed to rest, and supposedly threw rocks at the overseer. After appealing to Jefferson, Billy was allowed to stay at Poplar Forest, but a few years later, he had a similar encounter with another overseer. This time Billy, with the assistance of two other slaves, stabbed the overseer. Brought up on charges and tried in court, all three were sent to the Deep South, specifically to Louisiana's sugar plantations—essentially a death sentence. The other two slaves died within a few years, but Billy attempted to run away again, ending up in jail. No other information about what happened to Billy is known, but one can imagine that his fate was sealed. In the end, Jefferson only freed seven of the slaves that he owned at the time of his death.

Jefferson died at Monticello on July 4, 1826, at the age of 83. He left Poplar Forest along with 1,074 acres to his grandson, Francis Eppes, and his wife, Elizabeth. However, Eppes sold Poplar Forest to William Cobbs two years later and moved to Florida, where he founded Florida State University, following in his grandfather's footsteps. (Jefferson founded the University of Virginia in 1818.)

Cobbs's daughter, Emma, married Edward Sixtus Hutter, and the house remained in the Cobbs-Hutter family for the next 118 years. During their ownership in 1845, a fire broke out, burning all of the home's original interior woodwork, and it was subsequently rebuilt as a more practical country farmhouse. In 1946 the house was purchased by James Watts, who moved in with his wife and five children. The Watts family made significant changes to the interior rooms to fit their needs and owned the property until 1979, when Dr. James A. Johnson, a neurosurgeon from High Point, North Carolina, bought the house.

In the early 1980s, the Corporation for Jefferson's Poplar Forest was formed to acquire the historic house and nearly 50 acres of land. In 1986 Poplar Forest opened its doors to the public for the first time. The octagonal house, terrace, and its two outdoor privies are the sole original structures from the Jefferson era.

Encompassing 617 acres today, Poplar Forest is an architectural masterpiece. Although most of the original woodwork was lost in the fire of 1845, there is a special door displayed inside the house that is of interest. It was found covered in paint and sent to a conservator for restoration. Once returned, it was determined that the door was carved by none other than John Hemings. It is the only original piece of interior woodwork known to survive from Jefferson's time. Exquisitely hand-carved, its craftsmanship is remarkable. Whether visiting the historic house or walking the grounds, remember you are retracing the steps of Thomas Jefferson and the enslaved people who lived and worked at this site.

Central Virginia

Some of the first plantation homes built in this country are located along the James River, now a source of outdoor recreation and wildlife conservation that draws enthusiasts from all over. Its thriving culinary and independent music scene give it a harmonious ambiance that is unmatched elsewhere. Richmond, one of the area's largest cities, was also capital of the Confederate States of America, posing a beautiful juxtaposition of just how much things have changed over the last few centuries. Charlottesville is home to Thomas Jefferson's beloved University of Virginia (UVA) and is also a highly sought-after luxury destination getaway. As the site of some of our Founding Fathers' homes, this area is one where each and every step is truly a walk in early American history.

Appomattox Manor / City Point / General Grant's HQ

1001 Pecan Avenue
Hopewell, VA 23860
(804) 458-9504
www.nps.gov/pete/learn/historyculture/city-point.htm

A PLANTER AND HIS SLAVES

Appomattox Manor—also referred to as City Point and General Grant's HQ—was originally owned by the Eppes family, a 17th-century lineage that started with Francis Eppes Sr., an English immigrant. Serving as a colonel, Eppes acquired a large tract of land as a reward for his venture over to the New World. He settled along the banks where the Appomattox and James Rivers met, and his descendants would continue to live on the land for almost 350 years.

Built in 1763, the small one-and-a-half-story Georgian-style home started out with three rooms on the main floor and an unfinished second level. After Archibald Eppes died, he left the home, which had been passed on to him by his father, Richard Eppes, to his sister Mary, who married Benjamin Cocke. Their son Richard was born in 1824. As the plantation's heir, Richard received 1,700 acres, around 50 slaves, and the house at the time of his birth. But after Benjamin's death, he left the family in debt. Taking matters into her own hands, Mary sold slaves and other items to ensure her and her son's future and soon returned the family to their affluent status. When Richard turned 16 in 1840, his legal name was changed to his mother's maiden name, Eppes.

After finishing college, Richard pursued a medical degree from the University of Pennsylvania. While there he met the Horners, a prominent Philadelphia family. The Horners were known for patriarch William E. Horner's medical contributions to the University of Pennsylvania as a well-respected professor. Horner, a Virginian and once a student at the university as well, never left after marrying Elizabeth Welsh. The two had many children, including a daughter named Josephine Dulles, whom Richard married in 1850. The couple returned to City Point to reside.

Understanding the dangers of 19th-century childbirth, Josephine made Richard promise that if she were to die, he would marry her favorite sister, Elizabeth. Madly in love with Josephine, he initially protested, but later agreed. Possibly foreseeing the future, both Josephine and their baby died in 1852. Two years later Richard married Elizabeth, and they ultimately had nine children.

The house grew grander between 1840 and 1841 when Richard's mother, who dabbled in Gothic Revival, added rooms to the house. By the 1850s Richard expanded the western wing twice. Having honeymooned in Europe with both his wives, the Eppeses had many luxurious furnishings to decorate their surplus space.

As tensions slowly boiled over and Southern states began to talk about secession, Richard remained neutral, considering himself a conditional unionist, meaning he would support the Union as long as his livelihood, including slavery, wasn't disturbed. A detailed diarist, Richard kept meticulous records on his slaves and their occupations.

Occupation as well as sometimes favoritism played a part in the structuring of plantation slave hierarchies. For instance, James Madison Ruffin was one of Richard's most trusted slaves. Noted as a "gardner &c. [sic]," Madison, as he was called, had numerous duties outside of pruning the massive 12½-acre formal gardens, including managing other enslaved people, running errands, and even traveling to Baltimore and Philadelphia on Eppes's behalf. Madison was the only slave allowed to leave City Point for an extended period of time before the Civil War.

Madison married Harriet, the Eppeses' housemaid. Born on the plantation, Harriet already had five children and then had another six with Madison. All lived to adulthood. Favored by Eppes, Madison and Harriet received small monetary gifts throughout the year based upon their conduct, whereas the other slaves were only given gifts at Christmas (if Eppes was satisfied with their behavior over the year) or if they worked outside the regular dawn to dusk, six days a week. And though Eppes wrote that he and his overseers whipped people, about six slaves, including Harriet and Madison, were not to be touched.

Eppes did hire white workers for other tasks such as rearing his children, in addition to the two overseers who watched over the farming of wheat and corn as well as the tending of livestock. By 1860 the plantation's acreage had increased to 2,300 acres, along with 113 enslaved men, women, and children.

In 1851 the cook, Hannah Slaughter, born in 1786, was one of the oldest slaves Eppes owned. Her daughter-in-law Susan Slaughter, age 37, took over as Hannah grew older. Susan's niece, Ursula,

became her apprentice in 1857. Both Susan and Ursula accompanied Mrs. Eppes and the children to Petersburg upon their wartime relocation in 1862. While Susan and Ursula were away, most of the Slaughters were able to escape farther into Tidewater Virginia, around the Hampton Roads area. One of Susan's sons, Richard Slaughter, lied about his age to enroll in the 19th Regiment US Colored Troops in 1864. Ironically, he was stationed at the Bermuda Hundred property, which also belonged to Richard Eppes.

Another fascinating story surrounds laundress Sarah Calwell. Bought in October 1856 at the age of 22, Sarah was pregnant at the time. Unable to travel to the plantation during her third trimester, she had to wait until her daughter, Elnora, was born before going to City Point. Sarah's husband, William, was hired out by his owner to work in a tobacco factory in Petersburg. The two visited each other whenever possible. However, William wasn't keen on being enslaved and attempted to escape in 1858 along with four other slaves. Together they boarded the schooner *Keziah*, commanded by

William B. Baylis, a Delaware captain. Their plan to reach a location along the Underground Rail-road never came to fruition.

Twenty-six miles downriver, the ship was stopped by authorities and the five hideaways were found on board. The *Keziah* was seized and towed back to Petersburg, where all five slaves were punished and Baylis and his shipmate were placed on trial. Feigning ignorance about what happened, the shipmate was not charged with any crime; however, the captain wasn't so lucky. He and his brothers were known to help slaves escape, and his brothers were actually banned from even entering the commonwealth. Because of this, William Baylis received 40 years in the state penitentiary, 8 years for each of the slaves involved. Records show that Sarah still visited family in Petersburg after the trial, but it is not known if she saw William.

After the war broke out in 1861, City Point's location between Richmond and Petersburg made it vulnerable to Union troops. Shortly after Mrs. Eppes and the children's departure in 1862, the Union navy arrived and bombarded the area. The presence of the navy and nearby Union soldiers allowed 106 slaves to escape. Madison and Harriet were among the slaves who left but, oddly, later returned after the war.

From the summer of 1864 through the spring of 1865, the house was used by Union Quartermaster General Rufus Ingalls after City Point became the headquarters of General Ulysses S. Grant. Grant lived a few hundred yards from the house, first in a tent and later in a wooden cabin. Tactical in his approach, Grant understood that capturing City Point would give him an advantage in taking both Petersburg and Richmond. With railroad operations severed, Confederate troops suffered greatly, as their weapon and food supplies were cut off. This led to the beginning of the end.

After the Civil War, the Eppeses returned to their damaged home. Richard had to appeal to the federal government to get his house back since it was under Union control. Very few of the former Eppes slaves returned to the plantation to work. Among those who did were Madison and Harriet, with Madison staying until his death in 1876. Eppes requested that Madison be buried in St. John's Church cemetery and that upon his own death, his final resting place would be just a few feet away. The vestry (which Eppes sat on) obliged. Richard Eppes died 20 years later, in 1896, and was buried where he wished.

Not until the 1930s was the plantation house referred to as Appomattox Manor, one of the three names it has gone by. Eppes's descendants continued to own Appomattox until 1978, when the family sold it to the National Park Service (NPS). Over the last 30 years, the property has been turned into a museum. In addition to the house, there are four other protected outbuildings: an old smokehouse erected in 1820, a kitchen-laundry thought to be constructed between 1800 and 1825, and a newer smokehouse and a dairy built in 1840.

Appomattox's interior consists of a video room to provide more information about the Civil War, a room with exhibits on the Union military occupation, and two others that illustrate how the Eppeses lived. Various Eppes family members donated furnishings to the NPS. The grounds are just as intriguing, as not only does Grant's cabin still stand, but the vantage point of both rivers is gorgeous. Regardless of how one refers to the plantation, Appomattox Manor has been a thriving agricultural epicenter, stately home, and army headquarters and presently serves as a look into the past.

Ash Lawn Highland

2050 James Monroe Parkway
Charlottesville, VA 22902
(434) 293-8000
www.ashlawnhighland.org

HOME OF JAMES MONROE,
FIFTH PRESIDENT OF THE UNITED STATES

As you drive down Route 81 through Shenandoah National Park along Skyline Drive, if the mountains don't take your breath away, the changing foliage depending on the season will. Traveling this route is normally preferred to the hectic highway of I-95. Upon entering Charlottesville, a world of culture lies at your feet; however, the city may be best known for the number of presidents who built their homes in the surrounding area, be it Jefferson's architectural marvel Monticello, Madison's stately Montpelier, or James Monroe's splendid Highland.

Born to Spence and Elizabeth Jones Monroe on April 28, 1758, James Monroe was the second of five children. The Monroes weren't considered wealthy planters, but had a 500-acre homestead in Westmoreland County to grow tobacco. His parents made sure young James had the proper schooling, which prepared him to attend the College of William & Mary from 1774 until 1776. After a year and half at William & Mary, Monroe enlisted in the Continental Army's Third Virginia Infantry Regiment in 1776 and was wounded at the Battle of Trenton that same year. Continuing to serve, he spent a winter at Valley Forge and was present at the battles of Brandywine, Germantown, and Monmouth. In early 1779 Monroe resigned after the Virginia legislature appointed him lieutenant colonel.

Like many men of his status, Monroe decided to practice law and studied under the tutorship of Governor Thomas Jefferson. This prepared him for his lifelong career in politics. By 1782 Monroe was elected a member of the Virginia House of Delegates and a year later became a delegate to the Confederation Congress, serving for three years until 1786. During that time, Monroe met Elizabeth Kortright and they married February 16, 1786. The couple would go on to have three children—Eliza, James Spence, and Maria—though only the daughters would live to adulthood.

Monroe returned to the Virginia House of Delegates from 1787 to 1789 and was selected a member of the Virginia Convention, a group of men who would ratify the United States Constitution in 1788. Representing Virginia as a US senator, Monroe would serve for four years, from 1790 to1794.

In 1793 the Monroes acquired 1,000 acres in Albemarle County, Virginia, adjacent to good friend Jefferson's Monticello. Almost immediately after purchasing the property, Monroe was appointed by George Washington to serve as minister to France. The Monroes returned to Virginia in 1797 and began construction on their residence at Highland, but in 1799 James was elected governor of Virginia, serving for the next three years in Richmond.

After his term as governor, in 1803 Monroe negotiated the Louisiana Purchase as an envoy to France on behalf of President Thomas Jefferson. He then went on to become the minister to England and envoy extraordinary to Spain from 1803 to 1807. In the course of those four years, Monroe spearheaded many important achievements for the United States, including in 1804 negotiating the purchase of Florida from Spain. The Monroes witnessed the coronation of Napoleon while abroad.

Again serving as a member of the Virginia House of Delegates for another year in 1810, in 1811 Monroe agreed to serve as secretary of state for six years under another good friend, President James Madison. Never one to shy away from responsibility, he also worked as secretary of war for one year from 1814 to 1815. At the end of his tenure as secretary of state, Monroe was inaugurated as the fifth president of the United States in March 1817, a title he would hold until 1825. President Monroe is well known for his message delivered to Congress in December in 1823 that came to be known as the Monroe Doctrine, believed to be the United States' first foreign policy speech.

Throughout Monroe's time traveling abroad and to Washington, someone had to run the plantation's everyday operations. Using slave labor, 30 to 40 people worked the 3,500-acre plot. Highland, like many 19th-century plantations, had outbuildings such as saw- and gristmills, stables, a blacksmith shop, an icehouse, and a smokehouse. Field hands cultivated wheat, tobacco, and corn as cash crops. Monroe's enslaved gardeners also tended to orchards and vineyards. Domestic slaves would have had housing closest to the Monroe dwelling, while other enslaved laborers would have been spread out over the 3,500 acres closer to their occupations. The slaves who labored outside ranked lower in hierarchy than their counterparts who were either skilled or worked at the mansion. This is evident in the slave quarters, which varied in quality based upon their location.

Monroe favored the return of freed slaves back to Africa and the Caribbean, and supported the mission of the American Colonization Society, founded in 1817. Though this ideology never completely came to fruition, it was a popular concept during the early 19th century. Monroe, however, did not free his Highland slaves, instead choosing to sell them to an aspiring cotton plantation in Florida in order to free himself of debt. While he considered slavery an evil and supported the American Colonization Society, none of his own slaves would see Liberia with its capital hailing their owner's name: Monrovia. Despite his personal feelings on slavery, like most of the other Founding Fathers, he realized that arguing the point could and would tear the newly developed country apart.

After his presidency ended in 1825, Monroe served for the next five years as a member of the Board of Visitors at the University of Virginia, Jefferson's treasured institution. In 1828 he sold Highland to the Bank of the United States. Two years later his wife, Elizabeth, died and Monroe survived her by less than a year, dying on July 4, 1831, while in New York City. James Monroe's body was returned to Virginia in 1858 and buried at Hollywood Cemetery in Richmond, where President John Tyler and Jefferson Davis, along with other notable Virginians, are also interred.

Opened to the public in 1931, Highland's name was changed to Ash Lawn by subsequent owners, which is why both names are used today. The home was owned by philanthropist Jay Winston Johns and his wife, Helen Lambert, until his death in 1974, when the property was inherited by the College of William & Mary, Monroe's alma mater.

Today when touring, guests may be surprised to see contrasting styles and different types of architecture. That is because the part of the house that Monroe and his family lived in was completed in 1799. The eastern section of the house was added to the original Monroe structure much later. Architecturally, the older part of the house is considered a cottage. Though one story high, the four-room brick structure is enclosed by white-painted clapboards and has a fireplace in each room. From Monroe's study that houses many objects paying homage to his extended legislative career to the dining room which showcases furnishing from the time the Monroes spent in Europe, the house encapsulates almost 30 years of the family's residency. The Victorian wing built in the 19th century is not to be missed, as its rotating exhibits are fascinating.

Afterward make sure to walk around the plantation's grounds to take in the gardens, including a boxwood garden and seasonal vegetable and flower plantings. Here is also where you will find a regal statue of the former president. If you're fond of farm animals, they're around, too, and aren't shy about coming up to greet you at the pasture fence. Surrounded by beautiful, unobstructed rolling hills, Ash Lawn–Highland is a must-see while visiting Charlottesville.

Battersea Plantation

1289 Upper Appomattox Street
Petersburg, VA 23803
(804) 732-9882
www.batterseafound.org

THE LOST PLANTATION

Hidden in an industrial area among a neighborhood of houses built in the 19th and 20th centuries is Battersea Plantation. It is currently protected behind a padlocked gate, but the Battersea Foundation has great plans for this once stately Anglo-Palladian home.

The history of the Banister family, owners of the Battersea estate, is thought to have begun with Reverend John Banister, an Anglican minister and botanist. Born in England, Banister became interested in North America's flora and fauna while studying at the University of Oxford. As he submersed himself further into collecting specimens, he received funding from Robert Morison, his botanist professor at Oxford, and Henry Compton, bishop of London. Sailing to the Caribbean and finally Virginia, Banister was expected by Compton and Morison to assist in further documenting the colony's plants. He arrived sometime in 1679 and befriended William Byrd, a wealthy planter whose property was located along the James River.

Managing an area called Bristol Parish along the Appomattox River, Reverend Banister continued to serve as a minister and study his plants. He acquired 1,735 acres along the Appomattox River, at a place called Hatcher Run, and focused on attending to additional ministry affairs. In 1690 Banister met with other clergymen in Jamestown and assisted in laying foundational plans for the College of William & Mary. Although the death of Morison, one of his sponsors, had some consequential effects on his uninterrupted learning, John found time to marry Martha Batte, a widower and daughter of explorer Thomas Batte. Together they had a son, named John Banister II. Though it isn't certain exactly when Reverend Banister's son was born, it's unfortunately known that he wasn't able to enjoy his father for long. While out on an expedition with one of William Byrd's employees, the reverend was accidentally killed; however, there is no further information about how he perished.

Whether it was guilt or loyalty, the prominent Byrds of Westover raised John II, and with their support he too became a wealthy planter and befriended their son, William Byrd II. Entering into politics, Banister led an affluent life as a magistrate of Bristol Parish, and he accompanied William Byrd II and Major William Mayo on their expedition to lay out the cities Petersburg and Richmond Although it is unclear why John Banister is referred to as captain, he is considered one of the original executors of Petersburg.

Born in 1734, Colonel John Banister III was the next in line to receive the tract of land of his forefathers, yet his legacy lies in the accomplishments of his civic duties. Educated in England, he practiced law. Upon returning to Virginia, he married Elizabeth Munford in 1755, though it is thought that she died the same year. As a widower, John waited before he married again. His second wife, Elizabeth "Patsy" Bland, bore him two sons, Robert Munford and Nathaniel Banister. When Elizabeth died in 1778, Banister remarried again, this time to Anne "Nancy" Blair. She bore him another two sons, Theodorick Blair and John Munro Banister.

With so much land, various grains were cultivated on the plantation. Building an industrial complex of mills for both lumber and flour on the southern part of his land, John Banister continued to accumulate wealth. He even ran a bakery within the complex as well. Yet, as tensions grew and a revolution appeared inevitable, Banister shifted to coopering and manufacturing gunpowder in support of the war.

As a revolutionary representative, Banister supported the changes that were occurring between the Crown and its constituents. He was a delegate to the Continental Congress and assisted in framing the Articles of Confederation. Serving as a blueprint of how the nation's government should run, the document was sent to the original 13 colonies for ratification. Drafted in 1777, it would take another four years before all the colonies agreed to pass the articles in 1781.

John Banister's role in the nation's development made him an attractive candidate in local politics as well, especially in Petersburg, which became a town in the late 18th century. The only problem was that Battersea sat in neighboring Dinwiddie County, which prevented him from running for office in Petersburg. So the town redrew county lines to include Battersea, allowing Bannister to participate. He won the race, becoming Petersburg's first mayor in 1784. He died four years later and his estate was left to his oldest son, who sadly did not take over Battersea's affairs. Because of his actions, the plantation would have numerous owners afterwards.

The plantation's architectural history is divided into five periods: Period I (1768), Period II (1781–1805), Period III (1824), Period IV (1841–1847), and Period V (late 19th / early 21st century). Period I began in 1768, when John Banister III began construction of Battersea Plantation, where he lived until his death. Modeled after Anglo-Palladian architecture, the Robert Morris–style five-part home's assembly would later be copied by Castlewood, also located in Petersburg, built in the 19th century by Parke Poindexter. Battersea has a two-story central block with one-story wings connected by an east and west hyphen. Once completely covered in scored stucco, the Flemish bond brickwork now peeks out in several places around the house.

Period II's changes were subtle, such as turning the home's crawlspaces into cellars for additional servant space. Furthermore, the south-side portico was extended to almost include the entirety of Battersea's central block. Today the four-columned, two-story portico still remains.

When John Fitzhugh May bought the house in either 1823 or 1824, Period III commenced. Like the plantation's previous owner, May was a man of political stature, serving as a judge of the Virginia Supreme Court as well as other civic positions providing him a significant amount of capital. This allowed him the luxury of redesigning the home to his liking. Reconstructing Battersea to include more Federal-style architecture, this change enhanced its Palladian presence. Modifications included improving the window coverings and many of the exterior doors.

John and Catherine Waring purchased Battersea from May in 1841, which begins Period IV. Living on the plantation for only six years, the Warings did not do much. However, it is thought that the interior's Greek Revival design may have occurred during this time.

After the Civil War, Battersea, like many other homes, was left in a state of disrepair. By 1870 Franklin Wright took over the home and attempted to restore it to its previous glory. Period V saw the most interior alterations, with modern conveniences added. In 1985 Battersea was given to the

City of Petersburg by John and Carolyn McLaughlin Jr., and remained under city control for the next 25 years.

Facing south toward the railroad, the house still watches commercial trains pass by, as it's done since 1894 when the Norfolk Southern Railroad (formerly Southside Railroad) was built. The grounds held a handful of outbuildings, but only two remain today, the greenhouse and the kitchen.

Accessing Battersea requires an appointment with the Battersea Foundation, which acquired the property along with 35½ acres in 2011. Its interior sits completely bare, allowing one's imagination to run wild of how the home was formerly decorated. Within the entry, an elaborate Chinese lattice staircase wraps its way up to the second floor. Once highly sought after, this type of staircase was normally painted either black or red, but Battersea's is white. Currently its interior continues to undergo major renovations.

Raising funds and educating visitors about this historic home has been the Battersea Foundation's goal since it was acquired. The foundation is working toward discovering more about the Banisters and identifying slaves and other workers, as well as refurbishing each room to reflect either a certain time frame or owner. Excitingly, the Public Broadcasting Service (PBS) selected Battersea's grounds to film parts of their Civil War drama *Mercy Street*. Though the home was not the focus, the crew used an original cottage found on-site. Most recently, a $25,000 grant was awarded by Richmond's Roller-Bottimore Foundation to structurally restore Battersea's greenhouse, which is also referred to as an orangery. Thought to be built during John F. May's ownership, it quite possibly could be one of oldest surviving orangeries in the United States.

Educationally, Battersea's "Leisure & Learning Series—Life on the Lawn" incorporates seminars and workshops that focus on numerous topics such as art and history, war reenactments, and waterways along the Appomattox River, among many others. And there are social events, too, like an annual oyster and barbecue feast as well as a spring wine festival.

Battersea's future looks bright, as executive director Toni S. Clark is energetic and passionate about this diamond in the rough, and sometimes extraordinary surprises happen like Banister's descendants coming to tour. As the word gets out about Battersea, history buffs should be ecstatic to discover the connection between two great families: the Banisters of Petersburg and the Byrds of Westover. Meanwhile, as projects are completed, architecture enthusiasts further delve into almost 250 years of structural design. Soon those padlocked gates will be forever opened to the public for future generations to permanently enjoy.

Castlewood

10201 Iron Bridge Road
Chesterfield, VA 23832
(804) 796-7121
www.chesterfieldhistory.com

HISTORICAL HOME BASE

As raging fires burned Richmond to the ground, also lost were numerous original county records from around the state of Virginia. The tragic loss haunts historians today, as many were not copied. Little is known about Castlewood, but since its construction between 1817 and 1819, its unwavering presence cannot be denied. Its pale, buttery yellow shutter boards glisten in the sun's rays, contrasting against freshly painted dark forest green shutters, both colors reflecting its previous appearance. The long bricked walkway leading to its front entrance passes between two gas lampposts in the same shade of green as the door. This is the first impression Castlewood offers its visitors.

Thought to be born in 1779, Parke Poindexter hailed from New Kent, Virginia, born to George Benskin Poindexter and Sarah Parke. Upon moving to Chesterfield County, Parke and his new bride, Eliza Jones Archer, quickly settled into a farming-centric life. Parke served as a court clerk for the county from 1812 until 1847. In addition to his municipal duties, he also found time to farm his land. His name is listed in various volumes of the *Farmer's Register, A Monthly Publication*. Edmund Ruffin, president of the Virginia State Agricultural Society, established and edited the periodical from 1834 to 1842. Its purpose was to provide information dedicated to educating and cultivating the agrarian interests of farmers.

The new couple sought a humble abode, so Castlewood's building commenced. Parke Poindexter acquired the 180-acre plot from Henry Winfree, who received the land in 1754. Though the center part of Castlewood is thought to have been built in 1816, it is uncertain if it was already assembled when the Poindexters bought the acreage. Additionally, the wings differ in symmetry, as the southern wing is thought to be built on-site while the northern was built elsewhere and then moved. This contributes heavily to Castlewood's unique five-part design. Federal period in composition, the inside of the house gives way to molded plaster ceilings, some which can still be seen in the south wing. Most of the house is completely under renovation, making touring Castlewood all the more special.

After Parke's death in 1847, Castlewood saw many faces live within its walls before Trinity Methodist Church begin to manage it in 1860. Used as a residence for traveling Methodist priests, it was called the Old Parsonage until 1872. Afterward, the distinctive home greeted many more owners, with William Gilmer purchasing it in 1957. The Gilmers took on the massive project of restoration. Revamped to its early 19th-century glory, the home stayed in the family for 19 years, until the Heritage Savings Loan and Bank procured it in 1976. For four years financial transactions occurred, but by 1980 the county stepped in, operating it until 1988, when the Chesterfield Historical Society became the new owner. Ten years later, the society turned Castlewood into its main headquarters. Currently all photographs, maps, archives, and genealogical records are held at the Historic Trinity Church less than a quarter mile from Castlewood.

Little is known about Castlewood's black population, though we do know that in 2013 Florence Ethel Malone Smith, a black domestic worker of one of the previous owners, died at the age of 90. Nonetheless, exciting events have happened since it was acquired by the historical society. For starters, in 1999 a Virginia Commonwealth University archaeological dig turned up buried framework dating back to the 1700s, including a slave quarters as well as a kitchen thought to have been used sometime between 1770 and 1860. Mrs. Betty Wilkerson, the great-great-granddaughter of Parke Poindexter, along with her two nephews, Chris and John Sargent, came to visit in 2006.

In 2009 Pattie Grady donated the Castlewood Papers 1936–1957, detailing events during those years. With a Save America's Treasures $150,000 grant awarded by the US Department of the Interior National Park Service Historic Preservation Fund in 2011, continued repairs were able to be made, including the paintwork seen today. As projects carry on, aesthetics are just as important. With the landscaping company given an Award of Merit by the American Institute of Architects in 2014, Castlewood is a structure of beauty.

Peeking inside, its attractiveness is undeniable. Sunlight pours through its six-over-six paned windows enclosed by fine detailed molding, with the faux marbled mantel framed by the same feature. Look up, and the ceiling's cornice follows a symmetrical pattern. Take a moment to stop in the hyphen that connects the southern wing to the central passage. Here a four-step addition complete with a banister looks out of place, but it isn't. This is part of its idiosyncrasy. Upstairs is completely off-limits, as is most of the north wing; however, one can sense what this house once was and will soon be again. Before exiting, look closely at the door, which is original to the house. The lock, a quirky contraption, guards a house waiting to make its debut.

Considering that many of its neighbors have not survived, such as the Chesterfield Lithia Company, Castlewood's shift into the limelight has had a positive impact on its restoration. History once thought lost is slowly being uncovered diligently by the Chesterfield Historical Society. Descendants who return to its grounds have contributed little-known facts about the families who lived here. Coming full circle, the same church that offered a place of refuge to traveling ministers over a century ago now provides a home to the society and all of its 25,000 documents and 2,500-photo archive. Until further notice, this is where they will remain while the interior undergoes a necessary update that is about halfway complete. Its progression is one of anticipation and awe.

Eppington Plantation

14201 Eppes Falls Road
Chesterfield, VA 23838
(804) 748-1623
www.chesterfieldhistory.com

FRIENDS TILL THE END

Some of the greatest stories in American history stem from a friendship that developed between Thomas Jefferson, a Founding Father, and Francis Eppes VI, owner of Eppington Plantation.

Francis Eppes VI came from a lineage of men named Francis. The first was Colonel Francis Eppes, who arrived in the American colonies in the early 1600s. On July 14, 1637, the Crown granted him 1,700 acres in Charles County for the transport of his three sons and 30 servants from England. One of his sons, Lieutenant Colonel Francis Eppes II, was born in Henrico County, one of the first eight royal colonies of Virginia, in 1627. His wife, Mary Wells, birthed Francis III, who passed on the coveted name to his son Francis IV, who also continued on with the tradition, naming his son Francis V. There the tradition came to a halt when Francis V did not get married. As a result, his brother, Richard Isham Eppes, succeeded him along with the children he bore with first wife, Martha Cocke Eppes. Son Francis VI revived the lineage, and here is where the story begins.

Built by Francis VI, Eppington once sat on a plot of 4,000 acres, more than double the size of the land grant his great-great-great grandfather received almost 150 years prior. By the late 18th century, the Eppes name was synonymous with wealth. Francis VI's father, Richard, owned Appomattox Manor, also known as City Point, over in Petersburg.

Elizabeth Wayles was the daughter of John Wayles (father of Sally Hemings) and half-sister of Martha Wayles, who later married Thomas Jefferson. In his wife Elizabeth's honor, Francis began the gargantuan task of building the Georgian plantation home. The main two-story house was built between 1768 and 1770, while the exterior single-level east and west wings weren't added until 1790. The west wing held Francis's office. That year the first statewide census was conducted, confirming that Francis Eppes was the wealthiest man in Chesterfield County.

Though related to Thomas Jefferson through marriage, Francis and Elizabeth nurtured a bond over their love and appreciation of gardening and agriculture. Nowhere is this more evident than on Eppington Plantation. Owner of 125 slaves, the largest amount in the county, Francis relied on enslaved labor to take care of his varied crops, including tobacco. The plantation was only a mile and a half from the Appomattox River, making it easy to transport water to and fro. There, a gristmill stood, grinding corn and wheat into meal. Francis believed in diversifying his crops and produced peach brandy from his peach orchard, though he had other varieties of fruits. Without any of the original structures standing today, we don't know if a distillery and or winery sat somewhere close to the house, but it probably was a very happy place.

When Thomas Jefferson's wife Martha died in 1782, she left three motherless children: Martha, Mary (Maria), and Lucy. Distraught over his wife's death, Jefferson headed to Chesterfield to grieve, but soon learned that he was appointed minister to France. He decided to take Martha with him to Paris, leaving his other two daughters behind.

Disease ran rampant throughout the area, particularly a bout of whopping cough. Everyone in the Eppes household caught it, visiting cousins included. Heartbreakingly, Lucy Jefferson died at the tender age of two and a half.

Brokenhearted, Thomas Jefferson feared losing Mary. He wanted to move her overseas, but she was extremely fond of Eppington. The strong-willed 8-year-old, who mirrored her mother's beauty, could not be swayed by her father to move from her beloved adopted home. However, with her father having the final say, Mary, accompanied by Sally, traveled to join her older sister, Martha, and father in Paris. For two years Jefferson corresponded with Elizabeth, keeping her abreast of Mary's whereabouts. But by 1789, with the French Revolution brewing, Jefferson soon realized their safety was in jeopardy. He and his daughters returned to Norfolk in the fall of 1789, a few months after the storming of the Bastille.

Upon reaching Eppington, Jefferson soon learned he was being summoned once again to serve his country, this time as secretary of state under President George Washington. During this time, Mary grew fond of her cousin, John Wayles Eppes. And as her father's political career flourished, she sought the comfort of the Eppes family more and more. In 1797, as Jefferson assumed the position of vice president, he received word that his daughter and nephew were engaged.

John Wayles Eppes and Mary Jefferson married on October 13, 1797. The couple continued to reside at Eppington, along with Francis and Elizabeth, at the beginning of their marriage. Moving around to other plantations owned by the family, Mary did not return to Eppington until the birth of her first child, who did not survive past infancy. The next few years were a blur as she visited her father in Washington, DC, in 1802 and her sister in 1803, but she was never to return to Eppington. She died shortly after giving birth to her third child in 1804.

Archibald Thweatt, who served as a correspondent to Thomas Jefferson, purchased Eppington in 1810 and owned it until his death in 1844, whereupon he willed the property to his nephew, Richard N. Thweatt II. It was sold in 1862 to Henry Cox, another prominent Chesterfield planter. Both men owned a significant number of slaves while calling the plantation home, contributing to their wealth and personal well-being.

Fighting between the North and South raged like wildfire in the fields of Virginia, Chesterfield County being no different. The Battle of Drewy's Bluff occurred about 30 miles from where Eppington stood. Fortunately for the western part of the county, most of the combat took place on the eastern side, perhaps contributing to Eppington's unharmed appearance. The Civil War disrupted the agricultural way of life that had been in place for over 200 years. Many planters saw their farming operations suffer significantly, or worse, lost all that they had.

In 1876 William Hinds of Pittsburgh purchased Eppington from the Cox family. His descendants donated the house and 45 acres to Chesterfield County in 1991. Everything about the house is original to the Eppses' period. The Eppington Foundation works with Chesterfield County's Parks and Recreation Department to recount Eppington's lengthy history.

Since its acquisition, work had been done to restore Eppington to its glorious heyday. A paint sample was studied by an analyst from Colonial Williamsburg, who determined the mustard coloring in one room is an archetype to the house. The first floor of Eppington is available to tour during events such as Eppington Day or by special appointment; nonetheless, upon its anticipated completion (hopefully both the upper and lower levels), it will no doubt be a relished sight to see.

The Inn at Meander Plantation

2333 North James Madison Highway
Locust Dale, VA 22948
(540) 672-4912
www.meander.net

A STATELY HOME INTO AN INN

Why not stay in a historic home while touring other historic homes?

The beautiful and stately Inn at Meander Plantation sits atop a hill in Locust Dale, Virginia. In the early 1700s the plantation was owned by Colonel Joshua Fry, who led the Virginia militia during the French and Indian War. In 1991 Suzie Blanchard and Suzanne Thomas bought the property and created a 10-room country inn that also houses an award-winning restaurant.

Staying at the inn is like taking a step back in time while also enjoying modern conveniences and excellent service. Because of the inn's location, day trips to Thomas Jefferson's Monticello and James Madison's Montpelier are easy to manage. Guests also find themselves in the heart of Virginia's wine country, with perhaps the most storied vineyard, Barboursville (also once a plantation), open for wine tastings and tours, as well as lunches and dinners at the winery's restaurant.

While surrounded by history, the inn itself also has a story to tell. Originally named Elim, the plantation was patented in 1726 by Colonel Fry, who was a member of the House of Burgesses and a professor at the College of William & Mary. Elim was the first plantation settled in Madison County. Fry and his partner, Peter Jefferson, Thomas' father, surveyed and drew the first official map of the territory that included what eventually became the Commonwealth of Virginia. During the French and Indian War, Colonel Fry commanded the Virginia militia with George Washington his second in command. Fry died on his journey home from the Battle of Cumberland, and legend has it that Washington stayed for more than a month at the plantation to console his widow and children.

In 1766 Fry's son, Henry, enlarged the manor, and the property included 3,000 acres. Frequent visitors included Thomas Jefferson and the Marquis de Lafayette. Another visitor was William Wirt,

who in 1807 served as lawyer and counsel for the prosecution against Aaron Burr, who, although never charged for shooting and killing Alexander Hamilton in a duel, was eventually arrested and charged with treason. Wirt spent much of his youth at the plantation.

The mansion was spared military activity during the Civil War, despite the fact that it was only miles from Cedar Mountain, also known as Slaughter's Mountain, which saw one of the bloodiest battles during that conflict on August 9, 1862. Union forces attacked Confederate troops under the command of General Thomas J. "Stonewall" Jackson as the Confederates marched on the Culpepper Court House to forestall a Union advance into central Virginia. The Confederate victory was the first of the Northern Virginia Campaign. Look on the front of the property for the state historical marker that tells where Jackson and his troops crossed the Robinson River while heading to the battle.

In the early 1900s the property's name was changed to Meander, the original name of the river to the east of the grounds that is now called Crooked Run. The owner, George Shearer, maintained the manor as an estate for his two daughters, Judith and Julia. The sisters lived at Meander for the remainder of their lives. Noted international horse and dog show judges, they also raised championship whippets and corgis, as well as racehorses. They are credited with introducing whippets to America, with the Meander whippet setting the standard for the breed.

Following the deaths of the Shearer sisters, the house was sold to a land development company. After plans to convert the property into a country club failed, the house went back into private ownership in the 1970s.

Suzie Blanchard and Suzanne Thomas bought the property in 1991 and converted the manor and adjacent buildings into a 10-room country inn. Visitors pass through a white brick gate and take the narrow, winding road up to the inn's main building, located off the James Madison Highway. On both sides of the road, you will see grapevines. The inn still has a small vineyard producing Cabernet Franc, Petite Manseng, and Cabernet-Norton hybrid wine grapes. In addition, the inn's farm grows hay, corn, and soybeans. Once at the top of the hill, you will find the inn's grounds blissfully quiet, except for an occasional large and very noisy gaggle of geese flying overhead. Off in the distance, you can see the Blue Ridge Mountains.

The inn's reception area features comfortable couches and a gas log fireplace. The Lightfoot Room was named after the owners of the property during the Civil War, while the Dependencies

Building (formerly slave quarters) now houses the Robinson and Rapidan rooms. Suzanne said that when she and Suzie bought the inn, that area had a dirt floor and no water or electricity. A building across from the main house that housed the plantation's dogs was also converted.

The dining room is an intimate space with seating for around 20 people. On Thursday, Friday, and Saturday evenings, the dinner seating is at 7 p.m. The inn serves only Virginia wines, taking advantage of being close to so many wineries. The restaurant is open to outside guests, so this time provides an opportunity for guests to meet and greet in the inn's parlor. (During the week, guests can arrange to receive a three-course dinner basket that can be eaten in their room or, weather permitting, on the inn's porch.) Breakfast is an event at the inn, with seating at 9 a.m.

The Inn at Meander Plantation is perfectly situated for a perfect stay. Visitors may enjoy the historic setting, exceptional service, and expertly prepared meals while being a stone's throw away from nearby plantations and vineyards.

Magnolia Grange

10020 Iron Bridge Road
Chesterfield, VA 23832
(804) 796-1479
www.chesterfieldhistory.com

HOME, HOME ON THE GRANGE

Route 1 is a major thoroughfare running along the East Coast from Maine to Key West, Florida. Along the way, travelers pass by historic landmarks, extraordinary landscapes, and interesting route markers. Magnolia Grange, a graceful plantation on the outskirts of Richmond, is responsible for many detours. The beach can wait! Time spent touring this amazing plantation will provide fodder for additional conversations once you get back on the road.

Magnolia Grange has served various purposes and housed generations from three families. While the neighborhood has changed, the home stands tall and proud. Recognized as a county, state, and federal landmark, Magnolia Grange has been operated by the Chesterfield Historical Society since 1984.

In 1691 the plantation was part of a substantial tract of land owned by Captain John Worsham of Henrico County. He and his wife, Phoebe, had a son also named John and bequeathed the plantation to both him and his brother, William. For almost a century, property records of the land around the area known as Cold Water Run are murky, but in 1823 William Winfree purchased between 600 and 700 acres and built Magnolia Grange.

Once an active tobacco plantation, by the time Winfree took over, wheat and corn production was in full swing, complete with a gristmill located about a mile from the house. Local farmers used the gristmill to grind their grains into meal for profit. Winfree also ran the nearby town's tavern, providing meals and lodging to weary travelers as well as court attendees. The historic courthouse erected in 1750 was situated directly across from the tavern, also within a reasonable distance of the plantation.

The Federal-style two-story home was aptly named for the circle of fragrant magnolia trees that once adorned its front lawn. Painted white and visible from the road, the house was a pleasant sight to those visiting Chesterfield County. Also surrounding the home were large tobacco barns, an outside kitchen, dairy, and smokehouse. Remaining in the Winfree family until 1845, Magnolia Grange went through a series of owners until its last owner, the Honorable John F. Daffron Jr., entrusted the home to the Chesterfield Historical Society.

From the parking lot directly in front of the house, the home sits unassuming with its mixture of American and Flemish bond brickwork. Poised almost lovingly over Magnolia Grange is an Osage orange tree. The tree's bumpy, neon green fruit is inedible, but beautiful when collected in bunches. A lovely cluster rests inside a glass bowl in the home's entryway, creating a splash of color.

Floor-to-ceiling Zuber & Cie wallpaper adorns the front hallway in stunning murals depicting country scenes. Since 1797 Zuber & Cie has been considered the gold standard for painted wallpaper. This French technique uses more than 100,000 wooden blocks that were engraved during the 17th, 18th, and 19th centuries. Period carpeting covers the stairwell and floor, returning Magnolia's aesthetic to an early 19th-century appearance.

To the left of the hallway sits a parlor, its walls covered in dark wood, while on the hallway's right is a dining room where the family enjoyed evening meals. Each bedroom on the second floor is decorated to reflect the three major families that lived at Magnolia Grange. One room is a gentleman's room. There are homey touches like photos of the family, but the room's masculinity dominates. It evokes the feeling of a pool hall, with rich mahogany wood and dark green paint covering the walls. Pictures of William Winfree and his wife hang above the mantel, and a framed tavern license showcases Mr. Winfree's business savvy. What looks to be a card game not finished is sprawled across the table. A piece of paper and a quilled pen stand by, waiting to be dipped in its inkwell.

The Cogbill room holds a few special pieces, including a baby doll. Dresses perched on stands, all sewn by hand, signal the effort taken to construct such a garment. A crib at the foot of the bed is reflected in the extravagant mirror placed above the fireplace. Possibly the first baby monitor? Who knows?

The DuVal room bears witness to the many children that roamed the home during the family's time at Magnolia Grange. Two beds take up most of the room, a trundle bed hidden perfectly underneath. Above the room's simple mantelpiece, five pictures of the large family look out to inquiring eyes.

Listed as a Virginia Historic Landmark and on the National Register of Historic Places, Magnolia Grange hasn't changed much in almost 200 years, although it has been reduced to about an acre. Being in close proximity to the Chesterfield County Courthouse provided owners of the plantation with abundant opportunities for business and social events. In the early years, the plantation profited from growing tobacco, later shifting from an agricultural existence into one of politics. Regardless of household, one thing remained constant: the stateliness of Magnolia Grange.

Since receiving the home from Judge Daffron, the society has completed much of the needed restoration. However, there is still much work to be done. New carpeting is needed in the hallways and stairwell, in addition to painting the exterior, repairing crown molding, securing new furnishing for various exhibits, and basement and baseboard repair. Furthermore, one of the biggest projects is removing and replacing each and every window due to lead-contaminated paint. Awareness is created through public events and exhibits, incorporating school groups and Chesterfield County residents. Yet it is the staff members who keep the plantation's memory alive. With passion and commitment, they continue to document and explore Magnolia Grange's quiet history.

Monticello

931 Thomas Jefferson Parkway
Charlottesville, VA 22902
(434) 984-9080
www.monticello.org

PURSUIT OF HAPPINESS

Who was Thomas Jefferson? Bearing many titles, he is best known to the world as a Founding Father, author of the Declaration of Independence, and the third president of the United States. To the world of academia, he is the founder of the University of Virginia; to his family, a father and a husband; and to his colleagues, one of the most respected thinkers of his time. Monticello reflected all of these characteristics, as it was the place he called home until his death; however, to understand the house, one has to understand who Jefferson was and all that he stood for.

Born April 13, 1743, at Shadwell Plantation to Peter Jefferson and Jane Randolph, he was the third of 10 children. Eight years before his birth, his father purchased a 1,000-acre tract of land which would later become Monticello. Jefferson's father died when he was 14 years old, but that did not deter young Thomas's bright future, and at the age of 17 he enrolled in the College of William & Mary. Studious by nature, his course of study lasted for two years. During that time he developed a mentorship with his professor George Wythe, under whom he read law for five years. Wythe was a model for Jefferson, with a political career and a law practice. Their relationship would blossom into a lifelong friendship.

In 1764 Jefferson came into the inheritance left by his father but focused on his political career. He began practicing law by 1767 and served as a delegate in the Virginia House of Burgesses from 1769 to 1775. Within those eight years Jefferson met Martha Wayles Skelton, daughter of John Wayles and Mary Eppes. A young widow, Martha was courted by the 6-foot, 2-inch strawberry blond lawyer, and the two married on January 1, 1772. The young couple had six children, but sadly only two lived to adulthood. Receiving a large dowry from his father-in-law, including 11,000

acres and 135 slaves, Jefferson retired from practicing law. He did not rest on his laurels, however, as in 1775 he was elected to the first Continental Congress.

America was on the brink of tumultuous times as colonists began to loudly criticize Britain's heavy taxation. Divided between Tories, those who supported the Crown, and patriots, those in opposition, the future of the colonies was uncertain. And though the American patriots had an idea of how the colonies should be run, it would take a sense of direction and strong leadership for their ideologies to be recognized and executed. Men such as George Washington, the Marquis de Lafayette, and Patrick Henry began a journey that was unprecedented. As the American Revolutionary War loomed, Jefferson envisioned how to convey their message to the world. Drafting the Declaration of Independence in 1776, a document known for its inspiring language concerning the rights of man, his ideologies inspired a nation. Yet for centuries it remained a contradictory work, as its inclusion was reserved for certain people, excluding African Americans and women.

Nevertheless, this does not detract from Jefferson's stellar political career. Leaving Congress in 1776, he returned to his beloved Virginia and served as governor from 1779 until 1781. He continued his public service by becoming the minster to France in 1784, and during his five-year tenure, developed a deep appreciation of European culture as well as French cuisine. Following in the footsteps of America, the political climate in France was rapidly changing, and in 1789 their own revolution began. Jefferson returned to Virginia soon after.

Within a few months of arriving back in America, Jefferson heard from the commander in chief of the Continental army, General George Washington, who was elected president in 1789. President Washington requested the service of Jefferson as the first secretary of state of the United States of America. Later losing out on the presidency by only a few votes to John Adams, Jefferson became the vice president in 1796. He won the coveted title four years later, becoming the third president of the United States in 1801. Like Washington, Jefferson was elected twice, leaving office in 1809.

Like many wealthy planters of his time, Jefferson's land provided bountiful resources. The bricks required for the mansion were produced on-site, in addition to the nails and timber. The windows, however, came by way of Europe and Philadelphia. With 33 interior rooms upon its completion, the 11,000-square-foot mansion was Jefferson's pride and joy. Monticello's construction began in 1769, as a year earlier Jefferson had cleared a mountainside with visions of his new home. Moving into the South Pavilion in 1770, he lived there while the rest of the mansion was being built. He redesigned the entire house in 1796. The north and south terraces as well as dependencies were finished between 1801 and 1803. Work continued in 1806 on the North Pavilion, and it too was completed within two years. Altered to mirror the newly constructed North Pavilion, the South Pavilion was remodeled in 1808 and finished by 1809, ending Monticello's nearly 40 years of construction.

The countryside surrounding Monticello is stunning, especially during the autumn when the leaves are deep hues of crimson, gold, and burnt orange. Entering through the east portico, the entrance hall served as a waiting room and place to catch the breeze during Virginia's hot summer months. Depending on the time of day, light pours in, reflecting off the room's marble statues and elegant crown molding. One wall is covered from top to bottom with natural history specimens and maps, while to the right, another wall pays homage to Native Americans with various ceremonial pieces. Here you will also find an ingenious contraption of Jefferson's known as the Great Clock that tells what day it is by a weight system. To the right, the North Square Room's alcove bed was introduced by Jefferson as a redesign in the 1790s. Monticello's only octagonal room is also located on the north side. James and Dolley Madison frequently used the bedchamber, which is complete with an alcove bed and reproduction French trellis wallpaper. From here, the Northwest Piazza can be accessed.

Jefferson's dining room was exquisite, providing guests with a modernized experience. Chrome yellow walls and dining tables accompanied by self-serving stations made for intimate, lively dinners. Not wanting his guests to be interrupted, Jefferson installed a rotating serving door with shelves so that slaves could carry dishes to and fro without being seen. Additionally, another weight system would lift wine from the cellar to Jefferson and his dinner companions. After dinner, guests would retreat to the parlor, decorated in bright red drapery. Its parquet floor of cherry and beech wood was designed by Jefferson. Here entertainment could include a game of cards or playing musical instruments. Noted is the camera obscura, which led to the birth of photography.

The south side of the house served as Jefferson's private quarters, where he and his family withdrew from the public and engaged with more intimate colleagues. Whether in the South Square Room, used as a sitting room by his daughter, Martha Jefferson Randolph, or his private greenhouse located in the Southeast Piazza, this side varies greatly from the northern one. Yet Jefferson's library is magnificent. He was an avid reader, with the ability to read in several languages, and his library was adorned with rows upon rows of books. Jefferson sold the collection, totaling over 6,000 books, to Congress in 1815. His office, referred to as Jefferson's Cabinet, held objects such as telescopes and furniture and was conveniently located adjacent to his bedroom. One of the 12 skylights situated throughout the mansion allowed light into the bed chamber above his alcove bed; it is the same bed Jefferson died in on July 4, 1826.

One could not talk about Jefferson or Monticello without mention of his slaves. Trading and owning upward of 600 slaves throughout his lifetime, Jefferson's relationship with Sally Hemings is probably one of the most documented. Sally traveled to France with Jefferson's youngest daughter, who was left in the care of the Eppes family at Eppington Plantation after his wife's death. At some point Jefferson and Hemings's relationship developed and she became a long-term companion, bearing him several children. Her family members, including offspring, were the only slaves Jefferson freed in his lifetime. Perhaps one of the best-documented enslaved families in America, there is a Hemings tour available at Monticello on weekends.

Other families that lived on the plantation include the Gillettes, composed of skilled laborers; the Herns, who worked for Jefferson throughout his presidency in Washington; and the Grangers, also made up of skilled artisans and some of Jefferson's preferred domestic slaves. Interestingly, George Granger Sr. was the only enslaved person who would receive annual wages as an overseer. One of Granger's sons, Isaac, resided as a free man in Petersburg until the 1840s. His candid account of slave life on the plantation can be found in a publication titled *Memoirs of a Monticello Slave*.

Monticello's 5,000 acres was split into four farms: the house farm, Tufton, Shadwell, and Lego. Many of Jefferson's skilled laborers lived along the 1,300-foot-long road known as Mulberry Row. Foundations can still be seen where the numerous outbuildings consisting of dwellings and workshops once stood. At any given time, 130 slaves toiled at Monticello on a daily basis; however, Jefferson's views on slavery were that he disagreed with the practice but understood its significance to the success of the newly minted country. Monticello has done an excellent job of making sure that visitors to its website and grounds understand the role that slavery contributed to its history. Online exhibitions such as *Slavery at Jefferson's Monticello: Paradox of Liberty*, which examines commonly asked questions, and *Getting Word: African American Families of Monticello*, an oral documentation of families whose descendants once called the plantation home, have a candidness that is appreciated. Furthermore, building on 21st-century technological advancements, an application for your smartphone titled "Slavery at Monticello: Life and Work on Mulberry Row" can be downloaded.

Walking Monticello's grounds, it is easy to get lost in the expansive floral and vegetable gardens, as Jefferson grew over 330 varieties. His orchards boasted 150 fruit varieties, producing apples and peaches that Jefferson would distill into brandy.

Monticello is owned and operated by the Thomas Jefferson Foundation, founded in 1923, which oversees what is now half of Jefferson's original 5,000-acre plantation. Receiving no federal or state funding, much of the restoration has been accomplished by private donations, including work on Monticello's shingled roof, ventilation system, and outbuildings. Additionally, the foundation has established an educational utopia through its Robert H. Smith International Center for Jefferson Studies. Here scholars and researchers can submerse themselves in a world dedicated to Jefferson. Created in 1987, the Thomas Jefferson Center for Historic Plants' purpose is to preserve and collect varietals from earlier centuries, a horticulturalist's dream. If recreation is more appealing to you, head to the Saunders-Monticello Trail, an 89-acre park along the entrance of the plantation.

A wonderful historical and educational place to visit, it is no wonder a tour at Monticello can take up an entire beautiful Virginia day.

Montpelier

11350 Constitution Highway
Orange, VA 22957
(540) 672-2728
www.montpelier.org

HOME OF JAMES AND DOLLEY MADISON

James Madison was small in stature, but remains a towering figure in the history of our country. Known as the Father of the Constitution and the Architect of the Bill of Rights, Madison also served as the nation's fourth president, following his good friend Thomas Jefferson.

Montpelier, where a young James was schooled and later returned to live with his wife, Dolley, is now owned by the National Trust for Historic Preservation and operated by the Montpelier Foundation. From 2003 to 2008, Montpelier underwent a major restoration to both its exterior and interior. Visitors now are able to tour the mansion and grounds, not only to enjoy the beautiful setting, but also to learn more about a man whose intellect, passion, and hard work are largely responsible for establishing the longest standing representative government on earth.

James Madison' grandfather, Ambrose, was a planter who in 1723 received a patent for more than 4,000 acres in Orange, Virginia. To work the land, first called Mount Pleasant, Ambrose acquired 29 slaves. Ambrose would die when he was only 36 of what was originally thought to be a short illness, but later was suspected to be poisoning at the hands of three slaves who were charged and convicted of the murder. Two of the slaves were whipped but returned to Ambrose's widow, Frances Taylor Madison, while the one thought to be the ringleader was executed. Frances continued to manage the plantation with the help of her son, James.

By 1740 James Madison Sr. had added land to the original 4,000 acres and brought in more slaves to farm tobacco and other crops. He married Nelly Conway, who would give birth to 12 children, with only 7 living to adulthood. The couple's first child, James Madison Jr., was born in 1751 at Port Conway, the estate of Nelly's mother's family, known today as Belle Grove. James Sr. would build the mansion that would become the core of today's Montpelier.

While James Jr. always thought of Montpelier as his home, until his retirement after his two-term presidency ended in 1817, he spent little time there. After his death in 1836, Dolley continued to live at Montpelier for a short time, but financial difficulties finally forced her to sell the plantation and move back to Washington, DC. The property would pass through the hands of several owners, each making changes to the buildings and grounds.

In 1901 the property was acquired by William and Annie Rogers duPont, who enlarged the house, adding wings that virtually doubled the number of rooms to 55. They also covered the original brick with stucco. Their daughter, Marion, remained at Montpelier after her father died in 1928. When Marion died in 1983, she left a $10 million endowment to the National Trust for Historic Preservation and, in accordance with her wishes, her heirs transferred ownership of the property to the trust.

The National Trust for Historic Preservation took ownership in 1985 with the mission to return the property to what it had been during James Madison's lifetime. The Montpelier Foundation launched a $25 million restoration project, and the house now appears as it did in 1820. The stucco was removed, and the exterior's brick was restored and repaired. As with so many plantation restoration projects, authentic materials were used. About 80 percent of the wooden floors are original, along with 95 percent of the brick and 65 percent of the glass. More recently, the focus has been furnishing the mansion's interior. Furniture that was originally in the house had ended up in museums or in private collections, and efforts are being made to return those pieces to Montpelier. Research is being done to replicate the fabrics, paints, and wallpaper that decorated the home when James and Dolley lived there. In excavating one area, a rodent nest included a scrap of fabric which allowed curators to duplicate that window treatment for one of the mansion's rooms.

All of this scholarly work and painstaking effort has resulted in the preservation of an important part of America's history. Montpelier is to be treasured, not only because the mansion and grounds are magnificent, but because it was the home of James Madison, a Founding Father whose contributions continue to be studied and lauded. In some ways, Madison's career trajectory is astonishing. As a child, he was frail and often ill. Not enjoying outdoor activities, he stayed inside reading. Although Nelly homeschooled her children—a common practice those days in the colonies—James soon began to reveal his potential. At 11 years of age, he outpaced his parents. The decision was made to send him to study under a Scottish teacher, Donald Robertson, at a boarding school at a nearby

plantation. James proved to be an eager learner. By the time he turned 16, he could read and write six languages.

When James returned to Montpelier, his parents realized that they had a boy genius on their hands, and they hired a tutor to continue his education. At this time, fewer than 1 percent of the children in the colonies received any form of formal education, so the schooling James received was truly a gift, one that he would make good use of throughout his lifetime. James decided not to attend the nearby William & Mary College, but instead chose the College of New Jersey, the institution that would later become Princeton University.

John Witherspoon, a Presbyterian minister who was born in Scotland, emigrated with his family to become the sixth president of the College of New Jersey. Witherspoon transformed the college, putting in place many reforms and upping the entrance requirements. Under his leadership, the college would become a major outpost of enlightenment, competing with Yale and Harvard. He would also prove to be an important influence on James and other students, including Aaron Burr, who would serve as Jefferson's vice president; Philip Freneau, the poet; William Bradford, the second US Attorney General; and Hugh Henry Brackenridge, a justice on the Supreme Court of Pennsylvania who would go on to found the University of Pittsburgh.

In the 1770s revolution was in the air, and James would have certainly been affected, not only by Witherspoon, but also by his fellow students. John Witherspoon was a signer of the Declaration of Independence, the only college president to do so. James was an ambitious student, and he finished his four-year degree in two years. He went on to become Princeton's first graduate student, studying theology under Witherspoon. He also learned a seventh language—Hebrew.

Due to his poor health, James would not see combat during the American Revolution. His contributions would be more intellectual. In 1776 he helped write Virginia's state constitution, which became a model for the US Constitution. Although he was, and still is, referred to as the Father of the Constitution, he often protested that title, saying that the Constitution was not "the off-spring of a single brain," but "the work of many heads and many hands."

In 1789 Madison was elected to the US House of Representatives and helped write and pass the Bill of Rights, the first 10 amendments to the US Constitution. During this time, he lived in Philadelphia, where he met Dolley Todd, a young widow. Yellow fever had swept through Dolley's home in 1793, claiming her husband, John; one of their sons; and John's parents. Dolley survived, along with the couple's other son, Payne. Less than a year later, while walking down a street in Philadelphia, she was spied by James. Etiquette frowned on a man introducing himself to a woman, so James arranged an introduction through his friend, Aaron Burr. She was a beautiful 26-year-old; he was an accomplished 43-year-old, whose mindset was much younger. They fell in love, and after a whirlwind courtship lasting only five months, they married. Their union, from all accounts a very close and loving relationship, would last 42 years.

Dolley became the consummate hostess, both during her 16 years in Washington, assuming that role not only during her husband's two terms as president, but for Jefferson, who was a widower, and at Montpelier. During her lifetime, Dolley Madison was a huge celebrity. She was the first president's wife to be called First Lady, a title bestowed upon her in a eulogy by President Zachary Taylor.

When James Madison retired to Montpelier, he was 65 years old; Dolley, 49. The mansion was actually built as a duplex, very much the way townhouses are now configured, providing separate entrances and residences for James and Dolley and for James Sr. and Nelly.

The home visitors now enter has profited from the Montpelier Foundation's meticulous renovation. Notice the door and the vestibule, the oldest parts of the home, dating to 1760. A room on the first floor harkens to the Colonial period and once functioned as a receiving room for James's mother, Nelly. In the room is a table original to the home. This table, we are told, was where Nelly would place her bible and her sewing. Nelly lived to be 98 and died only seven years before her son, so she was able to witness his entire career and presidency, as well as enjoy many of his retirement years at Montpelier. Nelly's room, which originally was the only one representing the Colonial period, has now been refurnished to its appearance during Montpelier's general interpretive period, 1817–1836, as is the rest of the house.

Entering the drawing room, visitors certainly realize that Dolley's favorite color was red. The walls are lined with a rich ruby wallpaper, portraits of many Founding Fathers hang on the walls, and busts of notable Americans are placed throughout. While we think of these people as historic figures that we literally place on pedestals, for James Madison, they were his coworkers and close friends.

Listen on the tour as the guide recounts Madison's friendship with two presidents honored in this room: George Washington and Thomas Jefferson. Washington was 20 years older than Madison, but despite the age difference, they were very close. The first president was so impressed with Madison's intellect—commenting that he had never seen so much mind in so little matter—he asked the 25-year-old to be his first speechwriter. Madison would write President Washington's first inaugural address, as well as the House of Representatives' critique of the speech. The friendship between Jefferson and Madison spanned more than 50 years. Their working relationship followed a pattern: Jefferson came up with the ideas, usually a new way of governing, and Madison would figure out a practical way to make that idea work. That process would result in the Bill of Rights and the Constitution.

While you're in the drawing room, notice the games that are set up to be played. Besides a chess set and cards, there's a contraption with a handle that produces static electricity, giving the player a shock. As our guide noted, "There was not a lot to do in the 1800s."

For decorating the dining room, the Montpelier staff was fortunate to uncover an old catalog in which Dolley had likely marked the wallpaper she chose to cover the walls. The dining room provides a fascinating glimpse into what the Madisons' social life was like at Montpelier. Around the large table, the mansion's creative staff has placed life-size cutout figures representing the many

famous people who once shared meals with James and Dolley. Dinner parties at Montpelier often included 20 to 25 people (though the table now has fewer chairs). This retirement was not a relaxing one! Both Dolley and James had large families, with many brothers and sisters resulting in four dozen nieces and nephews.

Besides relatives, diplomats and politicians sought out advice from the Father of the Constitution. Others wanted to hear stories about the American Revolution. And because Montpelier was in a remote location, people didn't just come for dinner but would stay for days, even weeks or months. Dolley, in a letter to Anna Payne Cutts, on July 5, 1816, said, "I am less worried here with a hundred visitors than with 25 in W[ashington]—this summer especially—I wish you had just such a country home as this, as I truly believe it is the happiest & most independent life, & would be best for your children."

James Madison, at 5 feet, 6 inches and weighing between 100 and 110 pounds, was by far the smallest American president. Despite his reputation and accomplishments, he remained soft-spoken and introverted. At the dining table, he liked to sit in the middle so that he could hear and be heard. His writings indicate that he enjoyed these dinner conversations, calling them his "marketplace of ideas." No longer in Washington, even then the epicenter of politics, he now had to get his news from his many visitors. Dolley, the hostess, sat at the head of the table. No longer First Lady, Dolley's company was still sought after and people loved being in her orbit.

In addition to Thomas Jefferson, dinner guests represented by the figures around the table include James Monroe, the fifth president, who lived in Charlottesville and, along with his wife, was a frequent guest; Anna Payne Cutts, Dolley's younger sister, who, after her parents died, was adopted by the Madisons; Margaret Bayard Smith, a society columnist whose missives provide a wealth of information for historians; and Andrew Jackson, the seventh president, who, facing the nullification crisis in South Carolina, sought Madison's advice, even though the fourth president would have been 81 at the time.

One guest at Madison's table certainly gave the former president pause. The Marquis de Lafayette was an ardent abolitionist. To this day, many believe the American Revolution would not have been won without his help. He thought the new country would be based on freedom and equality, yet he saw that plantations owned by the Founding Fathers had slaves. Madison agreed with Lafayette, but he never freed any slaves in his lifetime. Standing against the dining room's sideboard, possibly hearing the table debate about slavery, is the figure of Paul Jennings, the enslaved butler who served Madison for many years.

The couple's upstairs bedroom is now furnished with the original bed, found locally and now back at Montpelier. The wood had been painted, but was stripped and refinished. Take notice of the beautiful fireplace mantel, thought to be a wedding gift from James to Dolley. The mantel is decorated with the goddess of fertility, reflecting James's aspiration for children. Unfortunately, he and Dolley were never able to have their own children.

In the newer part of the mansion is another library that Madison had built when he began having difficulty going up and down the stairs. Here he looked out at the Blue Ridge Mountains and worked on his papers, particularly the copious notes he wrote during the Constitutional Convention. Madison was the only delegate to be at the convention every single day and became the de facto secretary. The delegates had agreed that they would not publish their notes until after they were all dead, to stave off any debates about the writing of the Constitution. But Madison had a more important reason for putting together his papers—he needed the money.

Back then, there was no retirement fund for former presidents. Like so many plantations, Montpelier suffered financially, from depleted soil from tobacco, falling prices for wheat, and the funds spent to entertain so many guests. But perhaps the biggest drain on Madison's resources came about because of his stepson, Payne, who mismanaged the plantation. Payne also was an alcoholic and a gambler, and to keep him out of debtors' prison, Madison paid $40,000, a huge sum at the time. (A clerk would make $200 a year.) George Washington's papers had sold for $100,000, but Madison's, when sold to Congress, only fetched about $30,000, not nearly enough for Dolley to hold onto Montpelier.

At age 84, Madison's health began to fail. Suffering from arthritis and confined to bed or a chair, most of his days were spent in a small room off the dining room, where he could be moved for meals when not in bed. Though his body was failing, his mind remained sharp. Three presidents before him—Jefferson, Adams, and Monroe—had died on July 4, but Madison would die on June 28, 1836. Although Dolley was on the plantation grounds, she was not at his bedside when he passed. Two other people were: butler Paul Jennings and his favorite niece, Nelly. As he was nearing the end, Nelly asked him what was the matter. He replied, "Nothing but a change of mind, my dear." The entire country mourned, and the *National Intelligencer* reported that "the last of the great lights of the Revolution . . . has sunk below the horizon . . . [and] left a radiance in the firmament."

Dolley, who lived for another 13 years after her husband's death, loved Montpelier but was lonely without James. Dealing with her financial problems also took a toll. She moved back to Washington, where she remained a fascinating figure and was given an honorary seat in Congress. She knew 12 presidents, from George Washington to Zachary Taylor. Everyone wanted to hear her stories. During the last two years of her life, she may even have met Abraham Lincoln, at the time a member of Congress.

After Madison's death, life turned around for Paul Jennings, the butler. In 1844 Dolley was forced to sell all her property, including her slaves. Jennings was sold for about $200 to a local insurance agent. He then came to the attention of a northern congressman, Daniel Webster, who was secretly going around lending money to slaves so that they could buy their freedom. Jennings worked off his debt to Webster and after that was a free man. He was literate, having taught himself to read and write, and he wrote a White House memoir, *A Colored Man's Reminiscences of James Madison*, which remains in print. Landing a job as a government clerk in the newly established Pension Office, part of the Department of Interior, Mr. Jennings became an ardent abolitionist and one of the founders of the Underground Railroad. He also helped organize a slave escape, which failed.

Paul Jennings continued to visit Dolley Madison, who lived a few blocks from him in Washington. One story often told about Jennings speaks to his character: Knowing that his former mistress was now impoverished, he would leave a few dollars for her on a table as he left. When Dolley passed away in 1849, the entire government shut down, and President Taylor, his entire cabinet, both houses of Congress, and the entire Supreme Court attended her funeral.

After visiting the mansion, take time to enjoy Montpelier's grounds, which include 2,650 acres of rolling hills, horse pastures, and those amazing views of the Blue Ridge Mountains. Visit the Madison Family Cemetery, where James and Dolley are buried, and the Annie duPont Garden, a 2-acre formal garden with walkways, flower beds, an herb garden, and magnificent marble statues of lions.

One site not to miss is the Archaeology Lab, where you can see experts and students examining and cataloguing the many artifacts that have been discovered on the grounds. Four areas have been excavated pertaining to the lives of slaves: the Stable Quarter, the South and Kitchen Yards, the Tobacco Barn Quarter, and the Field Quarter. Early structures, including possible slave quarters, have been revealed. New exhibits cover the lives of slaves at the plantation.

Visiting Montpelier will whet your appetite to learn more about James Madison, a Founding Father whose legacy continues to inform and inspire the country he so loved.

Patrick Henry's Red Hill

1250 Red Hill Road
Brookneal, VA 24528
(434) 376-2044
www.redhill.org

HIS FINAL RESTING PLACE

Patrick Henry's Red Hill is a bit off the beaten track. Winding roads take you through sleeping towns while the wooded terrain gives way to small bridges tattered with age overpassing the Staunton River. The town of Brookneal was established in 1802, not long after the death of Patrick Henry in 1799. Advantageously located, Henry's ferry crossing transported people and goods such as tobacco. Beyond where the eye can see, beloved Red Hill awaits to share stories about Patrick Henry's final years of life.

The simple one-and-a-half-story house was built sometime around 1770 by Richard Marot Booker. His father was a colonel who served in the militia as well as the Virginia House of Burgesses with George Washington. When Colonel Booker died, he left a part of his substantial tract of land along with slaves to his youngest son, Richard. Attending the College of William & Mary, Richard Booker was one of the founding members of Phi Beta Kappa, the oldest honor society in America.

Patrick Henry acquired Red Hill in 1794 when he retired. Considered to be his favorite home due to its lush landscape, Red Hill was named for Virginia's red clayed soil. The plantation expanded from 700 to upward of 3,000 acres during Henry's possession. Dependencies stood all over its massive Staunton River Valley site, providing ample space and opportunity for a profitable agrarian life.

Quietly attending to his civic duties for over 30 years, Henry turned down many prominent political positions, including minster to France and Spain, a sixth term as governor, chief justice of the US Supreme Court, and secretary of state. He humbly served the common man without desiring titled recognition, embodying his modest personality.

Self-taught in law, Patrick Henry's persuasive orating skills (adapted from and inspired by Reverend Samuel Davies) garnered the respect of friends and the ire of foes. One of his first distinguished

acts of defiance came in 1765 when he proposed seven resolutions to challenge the unreasonable Stamp Act. However, he is most known for his patriotic "give me liberty or give me death" speech during the Second Virginia Convention where he openly opposed the Crown. This speech solidified his place in history, anointing him the "Voice of the Revolution."

The American Revolution hastily drew sides, even among patriots, and in the end those who fought for independence found themselves in a precarious position after victory. Leaders were needed, but only a few men were deemed sensible and trustworthy enough to be worthy. Appointed the first governor of the Commonwealth of Virginia, Henry would hold the one-year term a total of five times from 1776 to 1779 and from 1784 to 1786. After 1786, he did not run again and carefully chose his involvement in political affairs, yet he understood his contribution mattered significantly. A House of Delegates member until his retirement in 1791, one of his last acts consisted of garnering support for the Bill of Rights. Along the drive up to Red Hill, a row of seven flags flies, representing the seven states admitted to the Union from the vast territory that comprised Virginia in 1776.

The father of 17 children, Patrick Henry was a busy man. His first wife, Sarah Shelton, died at Scotchtown after her sixth child was born, following a battle with mental illness. He married his second wife, Dorothea Dandridge, a few years later. Together they had 11 more children, with the last two born at Red Hill. John lived into adulthood, but regrettably Jane died four days after her birth. Happily, two surviving daughters held their weddings at Red Hill.

Buying the plantation ensured Henry's ownership of a ferry crossing and warehouse once owned by Richard Booker. Ever the businessman, Henry leased both to Martel LeSeur, a French immigrant who served in the Revolutionary War. Red Hill contained myriad outbuildings and grew tobacco as well as wheat, corn, flax, and rye. An herb garden grows at the entrance to Henry's law office, east of the slave cabin, the only surviving structure from the time he lived there. The law office stands as a testament to his professional career. Here Henry found solace, as his rigorous pace had waned drastically after retiring from his law practice.

Once one of the most sought-after lawyers, Henry debated alongside greats such as Thomas Jefferson, George Wythe, Edmund Pendleton, and John Marshall. Arguing over 3,000 cases in his lifetime, the law coursed passionately through his veins. Henry continued to give advice to those who dropped by. The law office is actually two rooms: One has two beds and a fireplace, and the other, the main room that was used for his office, holds a map table, a pine ledger cabinet, and additional furnishings.

The Henrys' burial place is just a few yards away from the office. Here Dorothea and Patrick are buried. There is also a descendants' area where ashes can be spread over the earth if they so choose. When Henry died, he bequeathed his fortune to his wife and children, who would give him a total of 77 grandchildren. Son John Henry inherited approximately half of Red Hill along with the house. (His brother, Winston, got the other half.)

John had a son named William Wirt Henry, who went on to have five children, with four surviving him. He left the plantation to three of the children, excluding Lucy. He was thought to have done this out of fairness since she had married into wealth, but Lucy had other plans. She bought out her siblings and proceeded to build her own 18-room mansion in 1910, finishing it in 1911. But tragedy struck eight years later, when the mansion burned to the ground. Lucy really adored Red Hill, however, and moved into her great-grandfather's law office, where she lived until her death in 1944.

In 1944 the Patrick Henry Memorial Foundation was established through the efforts of James Easley of Halifax County, Virginia. Eugene B. Casey of Maryland provided the funds to reconstruct Red Hill. Using blueprints, the home was built to look as it did over two centuries ago. Respected architect Stanhope Johnson undertook the project. Changes were made throughout the property, but the foundation was careful not to disturb the Osage orange tree that stands between the law office and house. Deemed by the Virginia Forestry Department as the largest Osage tree in the United States, it is possible Patrick Henry sat underneath that same tree.

Red Hill plans to continue research on the plantation's slaves when funding becomes available. Upon Henry's death, there were 69 slaves at Red Hill . He willed equal division of his slaves among his children after his wife, Dorothea, chose her 20 first. Inside a reconstructed cabin behind the home hangs a photo that shows a man and a woman with the caption: "Uncle Harrison and Aunt Milly, Coachman and Housemaid to the Henry family. Served two generations."

Half a mile away on the plantation grounds is an African-American cemetery. To get there, you travel past a blacksmith shop and carriage house. Here the Quarter Place Trail begins, which replicates the plantation's agricultural history surrounding tobacco. There's a cabin, a tobacco curing barn, and an ordering pit. Keep going. You'll cross through a field and begin descending down a shallow ravine. Stones in varied shapes and sizes mark the graves and push through the mossy ground, letting their presence be known.

Before heading home, as this is an all-day historical excursion, enjoy some time inside the E. Stuart Grant Museum. Pieces owned by Patrick Henry and members of his family grace every inch of the gallery, including musical instruments, salt cellars, and even his walking sticks. The painting *Patrick Henry Before the House of Burgesses* depicts him delivering his 1765 speech against the Stamp Act. Taking up an entire wall, Peter F. Rothermel commissioned the piece for the Philadelphia Art Union. It was then acquired by Charles L. Hamilton, and his heirs donated it to the foundation in 1959.

Patrick Henry was a patriot in the truest sense of the word, but he was also a father, a son, and a husband. His skills as an orator helped lay the groundwork for this country. Realizing this, in 1986 Congress designated his home and burial place a national monument. Today the historic area includes 525 acres to enjoy.

Patrick Henry's Scotchtown

16120 Chiswell Lane
Beaverdam, VA 23015
(804) 227-3500
www.preservationvirginia.org

"VOICE OF THE REVOLUTION"

Unlike many of the plantations in this collection, the most notable resident, Patrick Henry, and his family did not build the home, but rather moved into it. Nor were they the last to live at the plantation known as Scotchtown. However, during the time that the Henrys lived there, Patrick was involved in the revolutionary actions we know him for today. Scotchtown was built in 1721, under the direction of Charles Chiswell, making it one of the oldest wooden houses in Virginia. Thanks to the efforts of Preservation of Virginia at Scotchtown, along with a few other stately homes that are covered in this book, we are able to take a step back in time and enrich our understanding of Colonial Virginia.

Charles and Esther Chiswell received the land grant for Scotchtown in 1719. Their fortune amassed from Charles's successful iron foundry and his career as a trading agent for the Royal African Company. William Byrd II toured his foundry at one point in time, praising Charles for his familiarity with his craft. Receiving a 9,976-acre land grant from Governor Alexander Spotswood in 1719, the couple was required by law to establish residency within two years. It is thought that Scotchtown began as a four-room home, built sometime between 1719 and 1721.

The couple's son, Colonel John Chiswell, a House of Burgesses member, inherited Scotchtown. While in residence, he had the house expanded to its current eight-room size. Colonel Chiswell and his wife, Elizabeth Randolph, had four children. The family lived on the plantation until around 1752 when they moved to Williamsburg, still operating Scotchtown as a working plantation. In an unfortunate series of events, eldest daughter Susanna's marriage to the speaker of the House of Burgesses and treasurer of the colony, John Robinson Jr., would forever mar the family name.

Scotchtown transferred in ownership to the Robinsons. However, John Robinson died in 1766, and here is where the scandal ensues. After his death, Colonel Chiswell discovered that his son-in-law had siphoned off huge amounts of money from the colony . . . some 100,000 pounds! This treachery, of course, angered many of the colonists. Chiswell became a target and was involved in a brawl, and he ended up killing a man. A mystery surrounds Colonel Chiswell's death, which is possibly the reason why his body is buried in an unmarked grave somewhere on Scotchtown's grounds.

After the death of Colonel Chiswell, Scotchtown was auctioned off to repay John Robinson's debts to the colony. Edmund Pendelton and Peter Lyons, executors, placed an advertisement in the *Virginia Gazette* putting the estate up for auction. The two took inventory of Robinson's possessions, which consisted of slaves, various livestock, and some 3,800 acres. Wanting to capitalize on their investment, they included a public slave auction at Scotchtown, selling upward of 250 people. Not a single slave remained once the sale was completed.

Up-and-coming lawyer and politician Patrick Henry purchased Scotchtown at auction in 1771. He moved his growing family, including his wife, their five children, and ten slaves, received as a dowry, to their new plantation home. Countless marriages were arranged in the 18th century, but Patrick Henry and Sarah Shelton's union was different, as they were childhood sweethearts. Sarah would give birth to their last child at Scotchtown. While the Henrys only owned the plantation for seven years (1771–1778), it is here that Patrick's political career took off. He rode from Scotchtown to Richmond's St. John's Church in 1775 to deliver his famous "Give Me Liberty" speech.

While Patrick's career was taking off, there were problems on the home front. After their sixth and last child was born, Sarah fell mentally ill, what today might be diagnosed as postpartum depression. Due to his loyalty to and love for his wife, Patrick refused to place her in a Williamsburg mental hospital. Thinking she would be more comfortable at home, she was confined to Scotchtown's basement under the constant care of one of their slaves. Sarah died in 1775, and Patrick remarried two years later. He and his new wife, Dorothea Dandridge, moved to the Governor's Palace in Williamsburg, where he served as Virginia's first governor.

It is uncertain what happened to Scotchtown in the ensuing years, but the house welcomed new owners in 1801, when Captain John Mosby Sheppard and his wife, Elizabeth, moved to the farm with their eight children. The home was able to accommodate their large family and their six slaves. The Sheppard family initiated many changes, adding a smokehouse, barn, laundry, and an attached kitchen. The interior of Scotchtown was drastically altered, with a change in the configuration of the rooms and the chimneys.

Remaining in the Sheppard family until 1958, Scotchtown was considered a historic treasure; however, the vast tract of land had been reduced to a mere 99 acres by the time of its last owners. Sold at auction, Preservation Virginia received the house along with 26 acres for $17,000. Shortly after, renowned architect Walter Macomber assisted in restoring the plantation home to its appearance when the Henrys resided there. Preservation Virginia has been around since 1889, operating as the oldest statewide preservation organization in the United States. Though not much is known about how each room was decorated, the house is furnished to represent Patrick Henry's residency. Opened to the public in 1963, visitors have come from all over to relive the Henrys brief time at Scotchtown.

Today the home stands as an eight-bay house, with the left side reflecting the residency of Patrick Henry and his family, and the mirrored opposite side displaying various artifacts of the Chiswell, Henry, and Sheppard families in a museum setting. Start in the museum area to review history from 18th through the 20th centuries. Next you'll pass through Scotchtown's narrow central passage, where summer breezes flowed and dances took place. Upon entering the east parlor, children's games are scattered around the floor while musical instruments sit on brightly upholstered checkered furniture. (Mr. Henry was said to be an avid fiddler.) Entering the quaint dining room, the space also includes a passageway to the attic. Though not open to the public, the attic is completely open, with beautiful exposed beams running the length of the structure. Each beam is specifically numbered to ensure its proper placement after restoration.

Only one bedchamber is furnished, holding a desk, a canopied bed, and a replica of the chair Henry died in at his home, Red Hill. The rare English court wig that sits on a small desk doesn't belong to Patrick Henry, but it is one of only three such wigs in the United States. In the corner of the west parlor, a copy of a map drawn by Patrick Henry's father, John, sits above an original map table used by John Henry.

You must exit the home to enter its basement. Here is where things become interesting. Descend the bricked steps, and immediately to the left you will see where Sarah was kept the last years of her life and where she died. A mannequin with a straight-dress stoically stands in the middle of the room. It isn't creepy or dismal, as uncovered beams and various windows give way to an open floor plan. Next to Sarah's room is a space staged as a slave work area. Next, there's a weaving room, where looms as tall as the ceiling sit, still used today. Pass through the wine cellar. Cool, but not damp, there is a ladder that extends to the first floor of the home. At one time the entrance to the cellar remained locked to restrict access to the highly prized vintages.

Parts of Scotchtown have resumed its agricultural past. Local South Anna 4-H cares for Hog Island sheep born at Mount Vernon on its pastures. Currently the sheep are amusingly named Martha, George, Old Man, and Ghost. Walk over to the animals and they'll come up and rub their heads under your hands, baaing loudly in approval.

Many families have owned Scotchtown, each making it their own. The white-painted wooden house holds many undiscovered mysteries. Yet Scotchtown's future appears bright as more and more people become interested in learning about a man who fought for liberty for himself and his fellow countrymen.

Tuckahoe Plantation

12601 River Road
Richmond, VA 23238
(804) 774-1614
www.tuckahoeplantation.com

BOYHOOD HOME OF THOMAS JEFFERSON

Tuckahoe Plantation is one of only two homes in this collection that remains under residential private ownership. This exclusivity alone contributes to its allure. The current owners welcome visitors openly, allowing tours of the facilities on a daily basis. You may be quite surprised that it unobtrusively stands less than a mile from the scenic, well-traveled River Road. Turning onto the graveled pavement, your silent trek begins. Cedar trees hover protectively over the driveway until approaching Tuckahoe in the distance. Staff buzz around the property energetically. As you step onto the grounds, it is likely you'll be greeted by house pets—one dog, one cat—both amazingly friendly.

Before walking up to the house, you'll pass numerous outbuildings which, like the property, are under permanent preservation easement to guarantee legal protection. Structures ranging from cabins to a smokehouse and a storehouse are along the path to the ivy-covered old kitchen. Peering inside, it still houses various accoutrements used in the past. Walk around the freshly painted white picket fence to the fruitful herb garden manned by a spunky and extremely knowledgeable gardener. Ask about anything growing and she'll give you a detailed rundown without blinking an eye, but always with a smile. A sense of excitement takes hold as plant-covered walkways open onto a plantation home built in the mid-18th century, thought to be around 1733.

The Randolph household was one of Virginia's first families and settled on Turkey Island, named for the abundant wild fowl. They had several sons, each of whom founded a plantation. Thomas founded Tuckahoe, the only one still standing in its original setting west of Richmond on the James River.

Located on the east side of the house, closest to the gardens, is the schoolhouse where Founding Father Thomas Jefferson attended classes at an early age. Born at Shadwell Plantation, young

Thomas moved to Tuckahoe with his father Peter, mother Jane, and siblings after the early deaths of Jane's cousin William Randolph and his wife, Maria Judith Page. The Jeffersons moved in, as requested by William's will, to care for the three orphaned Randolph children. They stayed for seven years. One of William's last requests was that his son, Thomas Mann, not be educated in England, but locally. Because of this the school was built just a few feet away from the house.

Barely 2 years old when he traveled from Shadwell to Tuckahoe, this journey was said to be young Thomas Jefferson's earliest memory. Along with his siblings and the Randolph children, they packed the one-room schoolhouse to begin to prepare for their future endeavors. Around Thomas Mann's 11th birthday, Peter Jefferson made the decision that he was old enough to run the plantation on his own. What a responsibility for Thomas Mann to bear, even with the help of trusted overseers. The Jeffersons departed to their cherished Shadwell, and son Thomas went off to boarding school and then William & Mary. At Tuckahoe, the juvenile Thomas Mann rose to the challenge with a certain sense of gusto.

Anne Cary must have been attracted to Thomas Mann's leadership, because the two were married and raised a dozen children together before her death in 1789 (the exact date is still visible, etched in windowpanes). Widower Thomas Mann went courting and soon married Gabriella Harvie, who was half his age. Gabriella bore him a son, Thomas Mann Jr., whom she made sure would inherit the plantation under her guardianship. When Thomas Sr. died, she married John Brockenbrough, a wealthy banker. They split the plantation into two tracts: Upper Tuckahoe, with the original house, and Lower Tuckahoe. Gabriella and Brockenbrough moved to Lower Tuckahoe and Upper Tuckahoe was sold to the Wights. Between 1848 and 1850 the Allens acquired both tracts and for the first time in over 20 years, the Tuckahoes were reunited.

Accounts of the plantation after Joseph Allen purchased it showed 994 acres which were planted with crops such as oats, wheat, and corn. Allen owned almost 60 slaves, purchasing his last five in 1859, two years before the Civil War broke out. A census of his slaves was taken on January 1, 1859, with names, ages, occupations, and, fascinatingly, shoe sizes. Out of those 50

or so, only six had family names: the Smiths, Randolphs, Parkers, Jimisons, Andersons, and Turners. Only five worked inside Tuckahoe house, including the cook and a single blacksmith by the name of Moses. More than 25 were under the age of 18, and the oldest was William Spurlock, age 57. Three enslaved children were born later during 1859, in June and July. Though one died, the other two, a boy named Willis and a girl named Idenia, couldn't have possibly conceived how their lives were to change in the wake of their freedom. Ironically, Idenia was born on July 4, America's independence day.

Joseph Allen left Tuckahoe to his son, Richard S. Allen. Unable to maintain profitable farming operations, the Allens faced foreclosure and the plantation was once again split and sold. The Coolidges, descendants of the Randolphs, purchased Upper Tuckahoe with 600 acres for less than $13,000 in 1898, and sold it in 1935 to Isabelle Ball Baker, grandmother of the current owners. Regrettably, the Tuckahoes would never again be reunited, with Lower Tuckahoe subdivided for a residential housing development.

Paying homage to family history, the childhood recollections written by Lalla Gresham Ball (Isabelle's mother) were published in a booklet by her great-grandson and simply titled *Reminiscences of Plantation Life in Virginia: From 1861–1865.* Poignantly she writes about four major feasts that would occur throughout the year. The first occurred sometime in the spring, after all crops had been planted, and was called the Feast of Planting. Afterward, during the summer months as harvesting began, another was held known as the Harvest Feast. By late autumn, corn shucking was of the utmost importance and given credence over anything else. Normally a huge celebration would be held, appropriately called the Feast of the Husking. As nights grew longer and temperatures dropped, cutting wood for the plantation's survival was the final and last hurrah for the year. Amidst its completion, the Cutting Feast ensued.

The amount of work needed to operate Tuckahoe's neighboring fields was intensive, but it didn't take away from the home's grandeur. Built in an H shape, it was unique for its time, as prominent Georgian features overshadow the Jacobean influence. The Jacobean style came into prominence during the early 17th century under King James I's reign. Known as England's second Renaissance, architectural accomplishments dominated strongly. Additionally, similarities between Roswell, a stunning plantation owned by Maria Judith Page's family, as well as the Peyton-Randolph House in Williamsburg, constructed by Sir John Randolph, underscore Tuckahoe's grandness. Original nine-over-nine windows adorn the home, whereas inside an ornate carved-wood stairwell greets visitors entering through the north door of the house. A better vantage point of the impressive woodwork is from the landing, but make sure to face south.

The Thompsons, present occupants of the home, live upstairs on the second level; however, the two north bedrooms and all of the first floor rooms are available to tour, in particular the white parlor, burnt room, saloon, and dining room. Each room has a special presence, but none as great as the saloon. Deep, opulent red hues of fabric drape softly around the room, while a grand piano sits in the corner with family photographs on top. In contrast, the white parlor, cloaked in its pristine lightness, reflects how women of the period were expected to be so proper in their mannerisms as well as in interactions with one another.

Tuckahoe's beauty is gently refined, thanks largely in part to each and every owner's upholding its regal originality. And as you drive away, knowing its history from Thomas Jefferson's presence up to now, it is hard not to shake your head in awe, recognizing that one of the greatest minds in American history was cultivated on these hallowed grounds.

Weston Plantation

400 Weston Lane
Hopewell, VA 23860
(804) 458-4682
www.historichopewell.org

A HOUSE BETWEEN TWO RIVERS

Weston Plantation is perched on the embankment near where the Appomattox and James Rivers meet. William Gilliam, born to John Gilliam and Elizabeth Poythress, was a descendant of an indentured servant family. William met Christian Eppes, who was a part of the Eppes family that owned large tracts at City Point and across the James River at Eppes Island in Charles City County, and in 1789 the two were married. Building their residence shortly after, the neoclassical Georgian-style mansion would be the first dwelling ever constructed on the tract of land.

Gilliam operated the plantation by growing wheat and potatoes as the tobacco era was coming to an end and planters were looking to profit from other crops. He was also involved in the shipping industry. It is unclear how many slaves toiled the soil and waterways at the plantation. Gilliam would later expand Weston, building two additional dependencies which probably were used as the laundry and kitchen, although those structures no longer stand. After William died around the turn of the century, Christian would go on to run her husband's business for almost the next three decades.

With Weston's location so close to Petersburg, the house did not go unscathed during the Civil War. The Wood family arrived at Weston in 1863, fleeing from Hampton, Virginia, after Union occupation. Their daughter Emma, who was 12 years old at the time, would later write *Notes on the Civil War: A Memoir by Emma Wood Richardson*, recounting her experience during the war. When the house was shelled by a Union gunboat, a cannonball was lodged between the first and second floors until it fell through in the 1970s. A replica is on display at the house today. Weston was also occupied by Union General Philip Sheridan, who used the home as his headquarters.

In 1869 Weston Plantation was sold to Philip Dolin, who came from New York City by way of Ireland to take advantage of the real estate downturn. The Dolan family would continue to work the

farm until 1922. As 20th-century industrialism took off, especially after the arrival of the DuPont factory in the nearby city of Hopewell, agriculture slowly died out at Weston. However, all was not lost, as the manor was acquired by the Broyhill family. The Broyhills would transfer ownership to the Historic Hopewell Foundation in 1972. Taking more than 15 years to restore the exterior and interior of Weston, the home was opened to the public in 1988. The foundation added two new structures in 2008, the kitchen and laundry.

Today the wooden house retains about 85 percent of its original moldings, wainscoting, floors, stairs, and chair rail woodwork. It is also the only surviving 18th-century plantation house on the Appomattox River. There is still much to be discovered about Weston Plantation, but its unspoiled attractiveness is what makes it unique.

Wilton House

215 South Wilton Road
Richmond, VA 23226
(804) 282-5936
www.wiltonhousemuseum.org

RANDOLPH RESIDENCE

Wilton House sits in a West Richmond residential neighborhood, moved from its original site in Henrico by the National Society of the Colonial Dames of America in the Commonwealth of Virginia in the 1930s. Built between 1750 and 1753, the Georgian-style mansion was constructed for William Randolph III and Anne Harrison Randolph. The Randolphs were a part of Colonial Virginia's ruling aristocracy. Their patriarch, William Randolph, began acquiring huge land holdings in 1680 and produced a number of heirs who continued to expand the family's wealth through their land holdings and civic and governmental positions. This permitted the family to own numerous plantation homes throughout Virginia.

With brick laid in Flemish bond, whether viewing the home from its river side facing the James River or entering by land side, its symmetry is duly noted. Nine-over-nine sashed windows, some original, are the soul of this two-storied house. Sans wings, Wilton is structured similarly to Westover, a neighboring plantation in Charles City, Virginia, and home to William Berkeley III. George Washington stayed at the home for three days in 1775 after Patrick Henry gave his famous "Give Me Liberty" speech at St. John's Church. In 1781 the Marquis de Lafayette made Wilton his headquarters before advancing with 900 soldiers to the battle of Yorktown.

Previously a 2,600-acre tobacco plantation that later shifted to cultivating grain, Wilton's interior is what makes it grand. The central passage, like other Virginia Tidewater homes, is flanked with rooms on each side. On the left side of the passage is a tall case clock, circa 1795, manufactured by Simon Willard of Roxbury, Massachusetts. Its deep reddish-brown mahogany is flanked by portraits of William Randolph II of Turkey Island and his sister, Elizabeth Randolph Chiswell, both painted by John Wollaston in 1755.

To the left of the central passage is a study decorated in a masculine style. On the right is an elegant dining room graced with Canton china; though not original, many of the furnishings are attractive period-appropriate pieces based on an inventory taken in 1815. Beyond the study is a bedchamber that looks out to the James River. The Chippendale mahogany bed with its blue-and-white-patterned bedspread provides a comfortable element. During the summer months in the 18th and 19th centuries, netting was draped over the furniture in a process known as "southern establishment" to ward off heat and pesky insects.

A black walnut stair banister leads to the second floor. Upstairs each of the four bedchambers has its own charm. The Randolph nursery, with its pristine white bedding draped over two beds and nearby baby furniture, possibly demonstrates how the family slept in private quarters. Across the hallway is a bedchamber reportedly once called the "blue room" due to its brightly hued pigment. This particular room holds a handsome canopied bed with a matching chair adorned with darkly

colored floral fabric. A few feet away, an English wingback chair upholstered in yellow appears sun-kissed as beams of sunlight stream across its seat and legs.

The house remained in the Randolph family from 1753 until 1859, with Catherine as the last Randolph to live there before marrying Edward Carrington Mayo. The couple sold the house to Colonel William C. Knight, who served in the Confederate army. After passing through subsequent owners, the Virginia branch of the National Society of the Colonial Dames of America acquired the home in 1933, taking special care to partially dismantle and reconstruct Wilton brick by brick in its new location.

Wilton House continues its dedication to preserving various collections, from a silk waistcoat thought to have been worn by Alexander Spotswood to the numerous exhibits put on by its staff. And though the rooms aren't individually accessible on Wilton's website, leaving much to the imagination, the house provides access to most of its furnishings online through the National Portal to Historic Collections. The ability to see over a thousand pieces from the 17th, 18th, and 19th centuries is certainly impressive. On our tour with Executive Director Keith MacKay, he informed us that previously most tours of Wilton revolved solely around the Randolphs; however, the organization has recently decided to include a broader aspect of the home's history.

With a mansion that was owned by such a prominent Virginia family, its undiscovered details leave us excited and patiently waiting. Hopefully, more information about its beautiful architecture, how it operated as a productive farm, and the enslaved people that worked there will be included in tales for future generations to come.

Chesapeake Bay

On a body of water that expands up to Maryland, this area's counties feature prominent names such as Westmoreland, King George, and King William. Rivers like the Rappahannock, Mattaponi, York, and Pamunkey weave their way through flat plains and a shallow inlet. Boats dock casually in front of riverfront homes and behind whispering reeds. Native wildlife is abundant yet doesn't disturb the area's tranquility. Chesapeake Bay is the largest estuary in North America and the second largest in the world. The area also is rich in history, beginning with the Englishman John Smith who, along with a small crew, mapped and documented the bay and its rivers from 1607 to 1609. In 2006 Congress designated the routes of Smith's exploration a national historic trail, making it the first national water trail. Descendants of the area's Native Americans live here and share their traditions, further enhancing the region's culture. The bay region saw action during the American Revolution and the War of 1812. Five plantations attracted our attention and are featured in this chapter: Belle Grove, Chelsea, Menokin, Rosewell Ruins, and Stratford Hall.

Belle Grove Plantation Bed & Breakfast

9221 Belle Grove Drive
King George, VA 22485
(540) 621-7340
www.bellegroveplantation.com

BIRTHPLACE OF JAMES MADISON

Located off James Madison Parkway is Belle Grove Plantation Bed & Breakfast. Not to be confused with a second plantation bearing the same name in the Shenandoah Valley, Belle Grove's journey into a bed-and-breakfast is nothing short of miraculous. Its water view faces the Rappahannock River, which flows south to the Chesapeake Bay. It is here that James Madison spent his early years. The house Madison grew up in is no longer standing, but its foundation sits below the current home seen today.

What started in excess of a 5,000-acre land grant known as Nauzem was given to John Prossor and Thomas Chetwood by Governor William Berkeley on November 14, 1668. In 1670 Prossor sold 1,000 acres to Captain Anthony Savage, who would own what was later to become Belle Grove until he died in 1695. Without a male heir, 700 acres passed to the captain's son-in-law, Francis Thornton, who had married his daughter Alice. Their daughter Margaret inherited the other 300 acres, which became a part of Milbank Plantation, after marrying her first cousin William Strother II.

From that 700 acres, Francis Thornton and his immediate family retained control of the plantation for the next century or so. After being sold to Elizabeth Thornton, the daughter of Francis and Alice Thornton and sister of Margaret Thornton Strothers, and her husband, Edwin Conway, the plantation was bequeathed to the Conways' son Francis. Francis Conway I wed Rebecca Catlett and they had at least four children, including Eleanor Rose "Nelly" Conway, born on January 9, 1731. Eleanor went on to marry Colonel James Madison Sr., born on March 27, 1723, to the esteemed

Madison family, the only son of Ambrose Madison and Frances Taylor. Although James Madison Sr. was an accomplished planter, it would be the son he and wife Nelly produced that they would be remembered for.

James and Nelly were based in Orange, Virginia, when smallpox broke out while Nelly was pregnant. Wanting to keep her safe, James sent her back to live with her mother, Rebecca Conway, at her childhood home in King George County. After giving birth to their son, James Jr., Nelly returned to Orange but left the baby with her mother until he was two years old, as the smallpox epidemic was still a problem. Fond of young James, Mrs. Conway left him and another grandson five slaves of their choice.

"Sawney," a slave from Belle Grove Plantation, traveled to the University of New Jersey (now Princeton University) with James Jr. Another slave named William, perhaps given by Mrs. Conway as a wedding gift to Nelly and James Sr., would accompany the future president to Philadelphia. James would later write his father explaining that he could not bring William back to Montpelier because he was too familiar with the idea of freedom. Because of this, James Jr. freed William. Destined for greatness, James Madison Jr. went on to become the fourth president of the United States, later residing at Montpelier, a plantation built by his father.

A historic town, Port Conway was named for Captain Francis Conway III, grandson of Francis I, in 1789. At the time, a ferry transported goods and passengers from Port Conway, an English shipping port, to neighboring Port Royal. The plantation soon changed families in a rapid succession. Francis III sold Belle Grove to John Hipkins, a shipping merchant located just across the river in Port Royal. Hidden below baseboards in a crawl space under the southern wing of the mansion are two previous foundations from the Conways' tenure. The current house was built in 1791 by John Hipkins for his daughter, Frances "Fanny," and her husband, William Bernard II, but it would take years before the 8,000-square-foot mansion would become what it is today with its 13 bedrooms and 11 bathrooms.

After Fanny died, William moved to Fredericksburg and remarried. Belle Grove was leased out until 1819, when William Bernard III and his wife, Sarah Dyke, moved in. When William died suddenly in 1822, Sarah and their two surviving daughters moved to Port Royal, and Belle Grove was again leased. In 1839 William Bernard II "sold" Belle Grove to William and Sarah's two daughters

and their husbands for just one dollar. They turned around and sold it to Carolinus Turner shortly after for $22,000.

A man of status, Turner made the biggest impact on the architecture of Belle Grove. He would not only add the curved doors on the carriage side, but also curved steps from England, curved porches, heart of pine floors throughout, and six-over-six-pane windows with lead glass that can still be seen today. When you walk through the mansion, the time period you are seeing is Turner's period of 1839 to 1872. When the Civil War broke out, Belle Grove was occupied by the Union, although Turner was a Confederate supporter; however, it went unscathed. But an outlaw did grace its presence.

After John Wilkes Booth assassinated President Abraham Lincoln, he and accomplice David Herold retreated farther into Virginia. They used the ferry at Port Conway to cross over to Port Royal. There the two holed up inside Richard Henry Garrett's barn a few miles from the port. The Union army pursued the fugitives and stopped at Belle Grove, where Lieutenant Everton Congar stayed inside while his men camped on the grounds. Later the detachment captured and killed John Wilkes Booth, who refused to surrender. David Herold turned himself over, was found guilty, and was hanged along with other conspirators in the murderous plot.

The Turners sold Belle Grove to John Tayloe Thornton in 1894. After losing interest in his investment, Thornton sold the property to a group that wanted to convert it into a vocational school for colored students. However, the party involved defaulted on the loan, and Thornton won his land back after suing them in court.

By 1906 Thornton resold the house to Captain John Fremont Jack, later lovingly called "Alfalfa Jack." Captain Jack was an experimental farmer from Los Angeles who came to Virginia to assist other farmers in replenishing the soil due to the harm caused by tobacco. He was extremely successful. At one point he and some of his peers rented a steamboat and made stops from Fredericksburg to the Chesapeake Bay instructing other farmers on how to do the same.

In 1916 Captain Jack sold the house to William Allen and Otto Brant, who transformed the plantation into a dairy farm. Allen bought Brant out after a few years to save his investment. Cows roamed Belle Grove's countryside until 1930 when Mary and John Palmer Hooker, a prominent real estate broker from Chicago, purchased the land. Restoring the home to its antebellum look, Mrs. Hooker worked tirelessly, even adding landscaping for her well-known garden tours. John and Mary lived there until both of their deaths, 1974 and 1981 respectively.

For six years the home sat vacant and deteriorated. The Haas family from Vienna, Austria, purchased the plantation in 1987. After working on other projects, the Haases finally turned their attention to Belle Grove in 1997 and began its lengthy restoration. Stripping it down to its frame, they rebuilt the grand mansion beam by beam. It took six years and $3.5 million but what stands today is a testament to their devotion to its historic value.

The Haas family decided to lease the property as a bed-and-breakfast, and on July 10, 2011, the Darnell family came across the advertisement. Two days later Brett and Michelle Darnell walked into Belle Grove Plantation and the beginning of their amazing journey. Through the efforts of the Haas and Darnell families, Belle Grove Plantation has not only become one of the top five-star bed-and-breakfasts in Virginia, but has opened its doors to visitors seeking a view of America's past.

Visitors from around the world have come to see an extraordinary piece of American presidential history. Four rooms are set aside for guests: the Madison, Conway, Turner, and Hipkins-Bernard.

They are all named for previous owners of the plantation—a way of honoring and remembering Belle Grove's past—and there's something special about each one. Upstairs to the right is the Madison Suite. Its royal blue walls with a reproduction of a naval junior officer patriot's uniform on display and eagle decor give the room a presidential feel. A single key lies next to the bed with the name Madison engraved into its tag. But it is the private bathroom that is particularly stunning. Separated from the shower, a deep clawfoot tub overlooks the river. Early morning soaks have never had such an appeal.

Across the hallway is the Turner Suite, elegantly furnished with an 1860 half-tester queen bed and yellow and salmon-pink drapes. The balcony faces west to the Rappahannock River, giving overnight guests a wonderful spot to view the evening sunset or to enjoy a cup of coffee while watching the bald eagles fish in the morning.

Head downstairs and turn left to enter the Ladies Parlor, where two gold settees invite visitors to sit down and get comfortable. If you've seen the movie *Lincoln*, you may recognize these settees since they were in the film, sitting in Lincoln's bedroom. The film won an Oscar for Best Set Design, so this is your chance to feel like a movie star.

A library filled with books donated by guests is treated as the gentlemen's withdrawing room. Handsome tufted leather furniture complement a statuesque chessboard as well as a drawing of Generals Lee and Jackson called *The Last Meeting* on the south wall and a colored photograph of General Grant on the north side of the room. To the left of the library is the Conway Suite. It too has a private bath in addition to a private sitting area. Painted a Colonial slate blue, it is one of the most popular rooms because of this color. The final room, dedicated to the Hipkins-Bernard family, is painted a light moss green. An 1820 Eastlake high-back walnut queen bed from Yorktown, Virginia, is impressive, fit for a queen (or king) with its detailed carvings.

Many of the pieces were purchased from antiques stores all over the state. Each was lovingly selected for its period style, and most come with a historic past that is described on the mansion tours. Artifacts found on Belle Grove's grounds are identified and dated by Ferry Farm's archaeological department. Ferry Farm is the boyhood home of President George Washington, located less than 25 miles away. Additionally, in partnership with the College of William & Mary, students take part in field studies for credit, with the artifacts returned to Belle Grove for display.

Michelle and Brett Darnell have many plans for Belle Grove. Three outbuildings dated between 1720 and 1750 will undergo restoration: the icehouse/smokehouse and the summer kitchen. Once the summer kitchen is completed, a slave memorial will be erected inside the sleeping quarters, listing the names of all who were enslaved. Since opening on August 1, 2013, Belle Grove Plantation Bed & Breakfast has received numerous accolades, such as being named the No. 2 bed-and-breakfast in Virginia by Trip Advisor. In 2015 *Virginia Living* magazine deemed it Best Bed & Breakfast, Best Special Event Venue, and Best Tourist Attraction Not to Miss.

There's something special about knowing a president once lived at Belle Grove as a little boy. The Darnells want visitors to enjoy the mansion, its artifacts, and the history of the plantation. Don't be afraid to touch, take photos, or sit on the furniture. The Darnells tell their visitors, "We love when people want to touch, experience, and ask questions about our pieces. History is supposed to be tangible, not stoic." When asked what makes Belle Grove Plantation so different from other plantations, they say, "Where else in this country can you stay overnight in a home that was the birthplace of a president? What makes Belle Grove different from other plantations? It's our human connection."

Chelsea Plantation

874 Chelsea Plantation Lane
West Point, VA 23181
(804) 843-2386

HOUSE OF AUGUSTINE MOORE

On the banks of the Mattaponi River, named for the Mattaponi Indians (one of Virginia's state-recognized tribes), sits Chelsea Plantation. The private residence was once the home of Augustine Moore, who immigrated to Virginia during the early 17th century. Moore became an affluent tobacco planter and acquired generous amounts of land in King William County.

After his first wife, Mary Gage, died in 1713, Augustine married Elizabeth Todd Seaton. The Moores had a few children but bequeathed Chelsea to their son, Bernard. Like his father, Bernard was a prosperous planter and also served as a justice of the peace as well as a delegate in the House of Burgesses. He married Royal Governor Alexander Spotswood's daughter Anne, and the couple were supporters of the Crown when the American Revolution broke out. Defying regulations and patriotic sympathizers, it is said that Anne continued to drink her daily cup of tea! The Marquis de Lafayette and his troops are thought to have camped at Chelsea in 1781 before the Battle of Yorktown, the most important battle of the Revolutionary War.

The home remained in the Moore family until 1870, when it was purchased by William Richardson Jr., a maternal descendant of the Moores. He came to own the property in 1959, and his wife, Ellen, sold the house to their son, William W. Richardson III, in 1973. A T-shaped house, Chelsea Plantation still retains its green hipped roof with Flemish bond brickwork lining its walls. As you walk into the 300-year-old house, its central passage is lined with walnut paneling and various antiques acquired by Richardson, who has transformed Chelsea into a living museum.

Though the second floor is unavailable to tour, the first floor has a wealth of history that Richardson is proud to talk about. Hanging on the wall in the library is a sizable portrait of William at a younger age. Museum-worthy period paintings look out over pieces of cream-colored furniture and an ivory chess board. Across the passageway in the drawing room, two striking pieces are not to be missed: a baby grand piano and a Gothic piece of furniture thought to date back to the 17th century.

Don't forget to ask to see two rare books from Richardson's library. One is titled *Voices of the Past*, highlighting prominent people of Virginia from its earliest days of settlement, and the other is *The Life of Sir Thomas More*, written by More's great-great-great-great grandson. You'll get goosebumps as Richardson handles each book as tenderly as a baby. Another pride and joy is in Chelsea's dining room. European paintings of royalty transform the area into a luxurious banquet room with polished silver kept in 18th-century storage boxes. With variously tinted china, salt cellars, and a handwoven rug, one can only imagine the celebratory dinners held here.

The acreage that surrounds the house is equally spectacular. Just a few yards from the reed-laced banks of the Mattaponi River is an immaculate wooden boathouse. Also, a huge pool that resembles

a scene from *The Great Gatsby* makes you want to take a dip during Virginia's warm summer months. Around the property, a number of outbuildings dot the landscape, including a schoolhouse and smokehouse. The barn was once used to film a horror movie, and there's a secondary cottage that may be rented by visitors. Enclosed by brick and iron is the family burial plot.

In 2012 William Richardson, recognizing the importance of Chelsea Plantation, turned the 568-acre property over to the Williamsburg Land Conservancy as a conservation easement. An assurance by the conservancy that nothing will be torn down, only repaired and restored, is something that Richardson supports wholeheartedly. Along with a staff, including Don Masterson II, Richardson keeps the 18th-century plantation running smoothly, as it is currently farmed by tenants. Once the home of Augustine Moore, Chelsea is a rare memorial to early Colonial history that needs to be seen, as it's a little piece of preservation heaven.

Menokin

4037 Menokin Road
Warsaw, VA 22572
(804) 333-1776
www.menokin.org

REIMAGINING A RUIN

Menokin is situated in the Northern Neck region of Virginia, an area geographically defined by vast waterways and open farmland. This once-thriving plantation is undergoing a strategic rehabilitation that challenges traditional historic preservation methods. Menokin was the home of Francis Lightfoot Lee and his wife Rebecca, the daughter of John Tayloe II, an extremely wealthy planter. Rebecca and Francis's marriage merged two powerful and affluent planter families.

Francis Lightfoot Lee was born in Westmoreland County, Virginia, and raised at Stratford Hall. He and his brother, Richard Henry Lee, were the only brothers to sign the Declaration of Independence. Although quiet in nature, Francis was serious about fulfilling his civic duties. He served in the House of Burgesses from 1758 to 1775 and in the Continental Congress from 1775 to 1779. During his four years of service to the Continental Congress, he and Rebecca left Menokin for an extended period of time to live in Philadelphia.

Menokin is an Algonquian word, and various spellings have been documented. The area where the Lees built their home, carved from the vast Mount Airy Plantation, had always been known by this name and they kept it. Rebecca's father financed the construction of Menokin as a wedding gift for the couple. With the house came a 1,000-acre tract of land and 50 slaves. Construction began in 1769, and during the two years it took for the house to be built, the newlywed couple lived at Mount Airy with Rebecca's parents.

The two-story Georgian-style house is thought to have been built by William Buckland, who is well known for his work at other great houses such as Mount Airy, Blandfield in Essex County, Gunston Hall, and the Chase-Lloyd house in Annapolis. The iron-infused sandstone used to build Menokin was quarried somewhere on the Mount Airy property. Using neo-Palladian influences,

Menokin closely mirrors Mount Airy's architectural design. The original presentation drawing of Menokin was found at Mount Airy in 1964.

Both Francis and Rebecca died in 1797 and are buried in the Tayloe family cemetery at Mount Airy. They left no children, and Menokin eventually became the property of Rebecca's brother, John Tayloe III, who later built the Octagon House in Washington, DC. Menokin eventually passed out of the ownership of the Tayloe family and changed hands a number of times over the years until it was purchased at public auction in 1879 by Alfred Belfield. Upon their deaths, Belfield and his wife bestowed the property to E. Stuart Omohundro, who had lived with them at Menokin since childhood.

Meticulous records were kept on the plantation's inventory, including Menokin's slaves. One enslaved man, David Gordon, saved enough money to buy his freedom. By 1882 Gordon begins to show up in tax records with an inventory of his own, including livestock, equipment, and personal items. Gordon family descendants still live in the area and are working with Menokin to tell their story.

The Historic American Building Survey (HABS), the country's oldest preservation program, was founded in 1933 with the purpose of documenting the architectural history of America. In 1940 the survey prepared a detailed report on the condition of Menokin—including photographs and 20 sheets of measured drawings—which served as a critical blueprint during the later restoration years.

Stuart Omohundro lived at Menokin as a recluse for many years. The decline of the economy following the Civil War and the Great Depression took its toll on the area, and few repairs and no improvements were made to the house. Abandoned after Omohundro's death, the house lay vacant for many years. A tree eventually fell, damaging the roof, and over a period of several years, the house began its slow collapse.

Omohundro's surviving siblings maintained ownership of the house, but nothing was done to keep Menokin in good condition. In an effort to protect what he could from thieves and vandals, surviving brother Edgar Omohundro removed the woodwork from the house in 1968. Local preservationists found a safe haven for it at Bacon's Castle in Surry County, Virginia, where it remained for many years.

In 1979 Menokin was designated a National Historic Landmark by the secretary of the interior. In 1995, in honor of his sister Dora Omohundro Ricciardi, Edgar Omohundro donated the house, the woodwork, and the remaining 500 acres of land to the newly formed Menokin Foundation. Led by the enthusiasm of Martin Kirwan King, Menokin's early rescuers worked tirelessly to preserve and stabilize what remained of the house and to interpret the history of the property, including the life of Francis Lightfoot and others who had called Menokin home.

Challenges presented by Mother Nature eventually led to the development of the glass house concept. In 2012 the foundation begin to search for an architect that could translate and execute their vision. The highly acclaimed architectural firm of Machado Silvetti in Boston was hired to lead an interdisciplinary team through the design and construction of a preservation effort known as the Menokin Glass Project.

Menokin is more than a historic house. The foundation's commitment to natural resource conservation and interpretation is fulfilled through its care and management of a vast and mostly untouched landscape. Of its 500 acres, 325 are under easement with the US Fish and Wildlife Service and are part of the Rappahannock River Valley National Wildlife Refuge. This area has been designated an important birding area and is home to one of the country's largest nesting populations of bald eagles. Its location on the shores of pristine Cat Point Creek, a tributary of the Rappahannock River and part of the Chesapeake Bay Watershed, has been recognized with frequent support from the National Park Service, whose Chesapeake Bay Office has helped develop a public access point for canoeing and kayaking on the creek. Menokin is also part of the Chesapeake Gateway and Captain John Smith Water Trail programs.

The unique approach toward the preservation of Menokin—both the house and the property—is challenging traditional ways of looking at historic preservation. In the spirit of revolutionary thinking that honors patriot Francis Lightfoot Lee, the Menokin Foundation is embarking on the most engaging preservation project in America.

Rosewell Ruins

5113 Old Rosewell Lane
Gloucester, VA 23061
(804) 693-2585
www.rosewell.org

LOST BUT NOT FORGOTTEN

Ruins such as the Colosseum in Rome or Machu Picchu in Peru are recognizable worldwide, but Virginia has a few of its own from its Colonial beginnings. There's always a story behind stoic ruins, and Rosewell is no different. Located just a few miles from Carter Creek, which empties into the York River, the hallowed brick shell of what used to be Rosewell Plantation sits silently behind not one, but two padlocked gates. Since its last fire in 1916, which completely gutted the home, overgrown vegetation and vandals have contributed to its ruination, helped along by its secluded setting, which is a bit off the beaten path. Regardless, the first time you see Rosewell, you will want to learn its story.

As exploration of the New World exploded, the Eastern Seaboard became Britain's pride and joy. Thanks to John Smith, the abundance of natural resources would benefit the settlers who came after him. Less than 15 miles from the Jamestown settlement, in 1639 George Menefie received 3,000 acres, a considerable amount of land, for his voyage to commonwealth. Producing a single child named Elizabeth, George left his entire land grant to her, which passed to her husband, Henry Perry, in 1645.

The couple had two daughters, Mary and Elizabeth, who both inherited the property. The sisters would go on to sell their land to John Mann in 1680. He and wife, Mary Kemp, would build the first known structure along Timberneck Creek. Through records of how the house may have looked, it is safe to say that Rosewell would later dwarf the original building in size. John and Mary had a daughter also named Mary, and when she came of age, she married Matthew Page. Between 1688 and 1689 the newlyweds lived on the Manns' land until John died in 1694.

John divided his land between his wife and his daughter, and it was on daughter Mary's plot that Rosewell would be built. Matthew Page died in 1703, and Mary waited almost two years before marrying his cousin, John Page, in 1705. A business-minded woman, Mary had John sign a prenuptial

agreement leaving her entire inheritance to the children she had with her late husband, Matthew. Mary Page died in 1707, leaving control of the mansion to John and her firstborn, Mann Page.

Four years later, in 1711, Mann Page assumed complete dominion over the property and married Judith Wormeley. Unfortunately, their marriage would be short-lived, as in 1716 while giving birth to their son, both she and the baby died. Page, possibly following in the footsteps of his mother, waited until 1718 to marry another Judith, this one a daughter of Robert "King" Carter, who was considered the most powerful man in Virginia due to his vast wealth. The couple continued to live in the house that Mann's parents had assembled, but a fire in 1721 would afford them the opportunity to build their own. It is unclear why construction didn't begin until four years later, but in 1725 Page began to lay the foundation of a mansion that was admired for almost the next two centuries.

In 1730 Page died, his fortune bequeathed to Judith. The mansion would remain uncompleted for another seven years, until in 1737 Judith received assistance from her father, allowing her to carry on with the construction of Rosewell. Their son, Mann Page II, completed the project sometime in 1737. Six years later Page II married Alice Grymes, and they were the first couple to reside in the grand home. They too experienced a short marriage, as Alice died in 1746. Following in the family footsteps, Page remained a widower for two years, until 1748, when he married Anne Corbin Tayloe, a member of the affluent Tayloe family. With debts accruing, Page began to seek permission to sell parts of his land and slaves to settle his obligations.

It is during this period that the first record of Rosewell's enslaved people was made. County tax assessments concluded that Page had 28 slaves at Roswell, with another 48 laboring at other farms owned by his family. Slavery was inherently a part of the Pages' history, as Mann Page II's grandfather, Colonel John Page, had worked in the 1670s as an agent for the Royal African Company. The company was a key player in the transport of Africans to the West Indies and Virginia, which would later be referred to as the Atlantic slave trade.

Moving with his wife Anne to Mannsfield, Page left Rosewell to his oldest son, John, and his wife, Frances Burwell Page, in 1765. John began renovating the mansion and while doing so was chosen to serve in Virginia's House of Burgesses. Commencing on what would become a dynamic political career, John was elected to Congress in 1789 and later became the governor of Virginia in 1802. He is the only other Page besides his father to have recorded the slaves he owned. In addition to their names and ages, John notated the occupations of his 35 slaves. Broken down, they were

grouped as 10 field hands, 12 domestic or skilled laborers, 4 elderly, and 9 children. The Page family would own Rosewell for over 100 years, until 1837.

It is important to speak about the architecture of the house before its subsequent owners, as the house would undergo major changes. Bricks laid in Flemish bond once made up Rosewell's three stories. Conceivably replicating the architecture of London, the plantation home had a basement and wings that flanked each side of its central block. Additionally, unlike many of the Tidewater plantations in the area, Rosewell's interior included mahogany and walnut instead of the commonly used Virginia yellow pine. However, in 1838 the house was finally sold outside of the Page family to Thomas Booth, who removed all of the paneling as well as the original roofing, replacing it with a gabled roof.

Booth handed the home over to his cousin John T. Catlett in 1847, and Rosewell continued to fall into disrepair. At one time the mansion was valued at around $4,000, but by the time Catlett gained ownership, it had dwindled to $2,500. Unlike his cousin, Catlett began to make his own renovations, enhancing the plantation's value to $6,725 according to 1850–1851 tax records.

In 1853 Catlett sold the house to Josiah Deans, whose family would own Rosewell for the next 125 years. Josiah's daughter Ellen and her husband, Judge Fielding Taylor, inherited 247 acres in 1904, including the home. Tragedy struck 12 years later, as a raging fire gutted the entire house in 1916. The Taylors' daughter, Nellie Taylor Greaves, received the land from her parents, but left it mostly untouched. Soon the home was unrecognizable due to overgrowth, weather conditions, and trespassers. In 1979 Nellie and her brother, Lieutenant Colonel Fielding Lewis Greaves, deeded almost 9 acres to the Gloucester Historical Society.

The Gloucester Historical Society began stabilizing the area around Rosewell and restoring its ruins. Due to the amount of attention needed for this project, in 1989 the society's preservation division became what is now recognized as the Rosewell Foundation, Inc. Before your visit, stop by the visitor center where a wealth of information is available, including a miniature replica of what the plantation was thought to look like as well as artifacts that date back to its prehistoric past. Rosewell is unique in that unlike Menokin, there's nothing left to rebuild, yet that is what makes the ruins so special: It's a blank canvas with an impressive outline, awaiting its debut.

Stratford Hall

483 Great House Road
Stratford, VA 22538
(804) 493-8038
www.stratfordhall.org

THE LEES OF VIRGINIA

A Virginia dynasty. That is what comes to mind when speaking of the Lee family, whose name is attached to some of the greatest movements in American history and aligned with other powerful ancestral names. But the family's influence came to an end before the 20th century began.

Stratford Hall, the birthplace of Robert E. Lee, embodies all that the Lees stood for. The Great House is vast, overlooking prehistoric cliffs rising almost 150 feet above the Potomac River. These cliffs, while imposing, are frail in composition. Part of the Miocene epoch, fossils from 15 to 10 million years ago are found everywhere. People from all over come to search the open riverfront for shark's teeth.

The plantation once included nearly 6,000 acres. A gristmill, built by Thomas Lee, stands roughly a mile from the Great House. Made from stone and wood, the mill ground corn and wheat that was later sold. Back in 1759, Stratford's strategic location near the wharf allowed the gristmill to provide another source of income to the Lees. However, its use declined, especially after the home was lost to debt. The gristmill was reconstructed in 1939 and updated in 2003 by English millwright Derek Ogden. Today the gristmill is operational on its original foundation. Flour and cornmeal are ground just as they were back in 1759, and those ingredients are available for purchase in the plantation's gift shop. Grits, anyone?

Other structures cover the massive property, including reconstructed slave quarters, coach house and stables, gardens, springhouses, the Lee burial vault, and a slave burial memorial. The Payne Memorial Cabin was built in honor of Wesley Payne, a descendant of a slave family owned by the Lees. When the Robert E. Lee Association bought the property in 1929, Mr. Payne was still living on-site. When he was asked what he wanted built to remember him by, he requested that the

cabin be built as a tribute to his family and a reminder to visitors that even in this beautiful place, many who lived on the grounds were not free. The association obliged and a few hundred feet away, tucked among the sweeping trees, sits the cabin, visible from Stratford Hall's river vantage side.

The history of the Lee family, which has been researched and written about extensively, continues to fascinate. To attempt to cover their story would take much more than the space allotted, but there are a couple of Lees who should be mentioned for historical context. It is Richard Lee I, the emigrant, who should be given credit for the Lees as we know of them today. Arriving in Jamestown sometime in the 1630s, he and his wife, Anne Constable, had eight children. The Lees returned to England, where the young ones could be properly educated, and while there Richard struggled with the decision of whether to return to Virginia. His business dealings in the New World continued to grow (he had about 16,000 acres in the new colony), and he felt it would be in the family's best interest to return to the colonies. Unfortunately, he became ill and died before seeing most of his family settled in Virginia.

Richard Lee II was the second son of Richard I and was considered a scholar by many of his peers. He displayed an intellectual's respect for learning, and his burgeoning library provided a rich learning environment for his children. Richard II outlived his wife but he died in 1714, leaving behind six mature offspring, including Thomas Lee, who was born in 1690. Envisioning how important trading would become along the Potomac, Thomas set his sights on "the Clifts," as the Stratford property was called in 1717. However, his family didn't live on the tract until much later. Living on Machodoc Creek, Thomas and his wife, Hannah Ludwell, had two surviving children, Philip and Hannah, at the time. However, in 1729 disaster struck as a fire broke out in their home, set by local servants. The family escaped but lost everything. Rather than dwell on their loss, Thomas became deeply involved in politics, thus strengthening the Lees' influence in Virginia society. They later moved to "the Clifts," renaming it Stratford for Thomas's grandfather's estate in Sussex, England.

Thought to have been begun around 1738 by master builder William Walker, the architecture of the Great House is magnificent. Perhaps influenced by structures in England or Scotland, the house is a two-story brick building with eight chimneys. Four generations of Lees lived at Stratford, with the first two living strictly on the upper floor and the latter two living on both levels. Bricks were kilned on-site. A testament to its materials, the house remains sturdy almost 300 years later.

The heir to Stratford, Philip Ludwell Lee, was a savvy businessman and expanded the Lees' wealth exponentially, growing the estate to almost 7,000 acres at its height. During his tenure about 200 slaves worked the land, but he also had indentured servants. David Currie was thought to have served the family as a teacher to Philip and his siblings. School was usually held six days a week, from seven in the morning to five in the evening. Though detailed slave accounts weren't kept throughout the Lees' ownership of the plantation, there are certain years that were recorded. Due to

the estate division in 1782, one account enumerates and names the slaves divided among Philip's widow and daughters, Matilda and Flora. Though viewed as property, the treatment of skilled laborers varied greatly from field slaves. Those with a skilled craft were given better clothing and housing, and, in general, led better lives.

All of Thomas's children, even his daughters, played a major role in not only Virginia but America's early development. Francis Lightfoot Lee signed the Declaration of Independence along

with his brother, Richard Henry Lee, who was vocal in his disdain of Colonial rule. The band of Lee brothers, along with George Washington and his brothers, signed the Westmoreland Resolutions (a document stating their grievances), evoking the passion and laying the groundwork of a soon-to-be new nation. Younger brothers Arthur and William Lee were never as well known as their older brothers, but they contributed through their positions in Europe as diplomats, actively writing pamphlets and spying on royal activities and reporting back to their brothers across the Atlantic. The two Lee daughters were also influential. Hannah talked to her brothers about women's voting rights, a novelty in 18th-century politics, and Alice allowed supporters and participants in revolutionary activities to use her home.

Thomas's brother Henry Lee also added to the family's appeal. Marrying Mary Bland, they went on to rear four children, one being Henry Lee II, father of Henry "Light Horse Harry" Lee III. Close to General George Washington, Henry Lee III is best known for two things: his excellence as a cavalryman and for his son, Robert E. Lee, who later attended West Point and became one of the most revered generals in the Confederate army. Henry Lee III and his wife, Ann Hill Carter of Shirley Plantation, lived at Stratford until 1810, when the family had to move to Alexandria due to Henry's financial disasters. Thomas Lee's placement of the main house, which is far from the river, protected it from being attacked during the War of 1812 as British troops patrolled the Potomac River, bombing and burning anything they could.

When visiting the house, guests enter through a side entrance, not using the stone steps. Stratford is truly awe-inspiring. Originally with 18 rooms and 16 fireplaces, the Lees' affluence is on full display. The Great Hall, measuring 30 feet square, hosted numerous dances and celebrations. The room, however, is the only one within the Great House furnished with reproductions rather than period pieces. Virginia yellow pine floors stretch the hall's entirety. Yes, the same floor on which the Lees walked. Lovers of books, please note that the room also held the Lees' library. However, when Stratford was sold in 1822 by Henry Lee IV to William Clarke Somerville, that sale also included approximately 3,000 books. These days, a number of Lee family volumes can be found at the duPont Library, the on-site research library.

In the nursery, a soft light hovers gently over where young boys and girls slept and played. A tea set and child-size chairs look almost brand-new, while a bed small enough to hold a baby doll is draped with dimity fabric. In the Blue Room, high ceilings 14½ feet tall provide a certain airiness. The mahogany cradle belonged to Hannah Lee Corbin, daughter of Thomas Lee, and was used for her children at nearby Peckatone (also known as Pecatone) Plantation. Further research on that site's inventory can be found in the Peckatone Papers. Floral fabric encases furniture and bedding, and period portraits and paintings dot the walls.

The schoolroom where the developing minds of the Lee children were educated illustrates the confinement of both teacher and pupil. Found on the first floor, a bedchamber is fitted with desks, chairs, and slates (as paper was considered a valuable commodity). On the way out, peer down into the brick-walled wine cellar that once housed multiple spirits from around the world as well as locally sourced Virginia wine.

After William Clarke Somerville's death, the property was sold to Henry and Elizabeth Storke. Mrs. Storke lived at Stratford for 50 years, until her death in 1879, leaving the home to her great-nephews Richard H. and Charles E. Stuart.

Mrs. May Field Lanier, the daughter-in-law of poet Sidney Lanier, began to raise the funds necessary to purchase Stratford in 1929—a daunting task, given that the Crash of 1929 happened shortly after Mrs. Lanier initiated the Robert E. Lee Memorial Association. The $240,000 purchase price was raised by 1935. Since then various projects have been completed. Recently, the parlor's carpet, loomed by the reputable Grosvenor Wilton Company in 2014, was installed.

Outside in the adjoining fields, hay and barley are grown. A herd of Red Devon cattle, which could have been found at Stratford centuries ago, lazily graze in the pastures. Highland cattle, sheep, horses, and goats roam around as well. Be careful of the llama who fiercely guards the sheep. There is also lodging for guests, scholars, researchers, and supporters of Stratford. A council house where members of the board host meetings is located just past the dining room, the Inn at Stratford Hall. Lunch is available daily and showcases Virginia Tidewater cuisine. Menu items range from The Gristmill, plantation-produced grits with cheese and a creamy tomato sauce, to the Northern Neck Oyster Platter. A couple of dishes pay homage to previous residents, bearing their names. The restaurant even has a version of a cronut! Who says plantation life isn't up-to-date with the 21st century? With no menu item costing more than $15, it would be a disservice not to dine here.

Stratford is always evolving. From observing winter birds with nature guides, to ghost tours after dark, to the annual Wine & Oyster Festival, Stratford continues to support its community through various cultural events, educational talks, and agricultural development. Though the Lees' descendants haven't lived on-site in nearly 200 years, it is probably safe to say that their vision of a profitable, working plantation is still in effect.

Coastal Virginia—Eastern Shore

The website for Virginia's Eastern Shore proudly proclaims: "You'll love our nature." So did the region's early settlers. The land, fertile and flat, is only 50 feet above sea level and produced ample harvests of vegetables and grains. And since the Eastern Shore is separated from the rest of Virginia by Chesapeake Bay, with the Atlantic Ocean to the west, there was also a bounty from the sea: oysters, clams, crabs, and many species of fish. Currently the Eastern Shore consists of two counties—Accomack and Northampton—and the waterfront communities include Onancock, Cape Charles, Willis Wharf, Wachapreague, and Harborton. There are also barrier islands, most famously Chincoteague, known for its annual wild pony roundup. Perhaps the Eastern Shore's separation from the rest of Virginia has created a certain mystique about the area's history and unique culture. Talk to the locals and you'll pick up an accent that linguistic experts say is very similar to that used in Shakespeare's London. The Eastern Shore of Virginia Historical Society, founded in 1957, has a yearly operating budget of $360,000 that helps to employ a staff of three full-time and three part-time workers, as well as supervising 20 volunteers. The society owns three historic locations: Wise Cemetery, Hopkins Brothers Store, and Ker Place, the plantation featured in this book.

Ker Place

69 Market Street
Onancock, VA 23417
(757) 787-8012
www.shorehistory.org

A GEM TUCKED ALONG THE EASTERN SHORE

A thick fog blankets the sleepy town of Onancock, Virginia, once referred to as the Port of Scarborough. Founded in 1680, it was initially settled by the Scarborough family from England around 1628 and over time grew in population as an influx of colonists came over to the New World. Tucked along the inland coastline of Chesapeake Bay, Onancock is currently reachable by Onancock Creek or Route 13, and whether you chose to access the area by way of Maryland or Virginia, it remains one of the most picturesque glimpses into early American Colonial history.

With a square area a little over 1 mile, Onancock is small by any means, but its position in the county of Accomack solidifies its historical lineage. One of the first original eight colonies of Virginia, Accomack was founded in 1634, only later to be spilt into two sectors in 1663. Almost a century after its development, Edward Ker of Cessford, Scotland, arrived along the Eastern Shore of Virginia sometime in the early 1750s, marrying Margaret Shepard circa 1753. After buying a large tract of land along the shoreline, the property was divided among his family upon his death in 1790. In his will, he gave his son, John Shepherd Ker, more than 300 acres of land.

John Ker married Agnes Drummond Corbin, the daughter of another prominent family living in the area. Given additional acreage by the Corbins after their marriage, the young couple originally lived in Scott Hall, another property owned by the Corbin family. Deemed the oldest house in the area, John and Agnes resided in Scott Hall for a few years while Ker Place was constructed.

Built between 1799 and 1801, the Federal-style home is considered the finest example on the Eastern Shore of Virginia. Behind its white fence, it showcases the evolution of change from Colonial America's interest in the Georgian style to Federal. Robert Adam created the new style by taking into consideration the styles of Roman and Greek architecture; however, it was Charles Bulfinch who is credited with bringing the Federal style to the United States. Yet as the style started to draw interest, it was Asher Benjamin's pattern book that inspired various carpenters and builders along the Eastern Seaboard, who introduced it to the masses.

Mrs. Ker's desire to showcase the family's wealth is reflected in small details within the house. Upon entering the structure, perched in the attic is an oculus window, a luxury at that time. The window along with doors and plaster molding have Virginia's state flower, the American dogwood, carved in them. White in color, the American dogwood is native to eastern North America, found as far north as Ontario and as far south as Florida. Another quirky addition is the faux-marble paneling alongside the baseboards. Gray with black swirling, it appears to be the real thing; however, the cost of such detail would have been quite expensive. Instead the ever-crafty Mrs. Ker paid someone to hand paint the house in its entirety, giving off an elegant appearance. Mr. Ker contributed to its look as well. Utilitarian in nature, pegs are hammered into the entry hall to hang articles of clothing.

Self-sufficient, as most plantation homes were, the home's bricks and mortar were produced on-site. Made from the abundance of oyster shells found nearby, the mortar was cooked down and mixed with sand to produce a limestone-like mixture. Additionally, light was provided by home-made candles located throughout the house. Whether it was a candle maker or slave, that person's job was quite tedious since light was always needed by the family, especially at night. Each candelabra required constant attention, with candles being changed up to 40 times a day! Fat from the animals allowed a steady flow of candles to be prepared and burned.

John Ker considered himself a Federalist, serving in a militia during the Revolutionary War. It is said that a cellarette full of Chincoteague oysters, brandy, and smoked meats from the Eastern Shore's countryside was sent to George Washington and his men stationed along the Delaware River. A cellarette is a wooden or leather trunk that contains compartments to place various goods. After regaining their strength, Washington's men went on to defeat the British army.

The Kers were slave owners. Though much is still being researched, in August of 1806, before his death, John Ker named five slaves to be freed in 1808 in his will. In the same document he additionally requested that between the years 1810 and 1826, an additional eight slaves be released. Though the freeing of slaves was not uncommon, releasing so many profitable slaves was, especially since John and Agnes had an heir, Edward H. Ker. Perhaps John took after his father-in-law, George Corbin, who manumitted 14 slaves in 1787.

Due to its location, the Eastern Shore and its homes were able to escape many aspects of war, including the topic of slavery. Virginia seceded on April 4, 1861, and the Civil War broke out a mere eight days later. However, what may not be known is that the Commonwealth of Virginia had two capitals. While Richmond was named capital of the Confederate states, Wheeling, Virginia (now West Virginia), was considered by western and eastern counties to be their capital. Recognized by President Abraham Lincoln as loyalists, the Eastern Shore and their counterparts were a part of the Union. Not until 1863 did things change as the western counties continued to push for statehood, and on June 20, in the midst of the Civil War, West Virginia was formed.

Wheat, corn, and castor beans were grown on the Ker plantation. The wheat and corn were used for both human and animal consumption, while the castor beans had a more practical use. Ground and processed into oil, it then was used to lubricate machinery on the plantation as well as leather goods.

Without the presence of banks, Mr. Ker, because of his stature, was able to act as a bank. Tenants of smaller farms were loaned specified amounts of money to be paid by their promised dates. John Ker was not only a farmer but had his hands in a bit of everything. As a merchant, his ties to the shipping industry allowed him the opportunity to take others' crops and goods to trading ports such as Baltimore.

John Ker died in 1806, his wife in 1814. The house never transferred out of the Ker family, as his sister Margaret S. Ker, who'd married Smith U. Snead, had a son by the name of Edward Smith Snead. It remained in the Snead family until 1875, when it was purchased by George W. Powell. For the next 85 years, the Powell family called Ker Place home and finally in 1960 granted ownership to the Eastern Shore of Virginia Historical Society. By 1969 Ker Place made the Virginia Landmarks Register and was listed on the National Register of Historic Places in 1970.

Currently serving as a museum, the first floor preserves its early national as well as pre–Civil War history. However, Ker Place is resilient. Walking up to the second floor, the home becomes a museum paying homage to General John Cropper, who fought in the Revolutionary War until 1778, before returning back home to care for his family and serve as a colonel of the Virginia militia of Accomack County.

Henry A. Wise, a governor of Virginia (1856–1860), is also highlighted. Though born in Accomack County, Wise is known for the critical decision he made regarding the fate of John Brown,

the abolitionist who incited the slave rebellion in Harpers Ferry. Instead of commuting Brown's sentence, he allowed the execution to occur.

Below in the basement, original brickwork makes up the floor. Chairs woven by slaves along with other pieces of furniture sit quietly undisturbed. Glass-enclosed containers hold broken dishes, among other artifacts found on the grounds. The connectivity of Virginia's plantations is noted as a wall placement provides historical background on Francis Makemie, founder of American Presbyterianism. Purchasing land in Accomack County in 1687, he later was appointed by Governor Francis Nicholson and eight other council members from the colony of Virginia to be the first nonconforming minister outside the Church of England. One of those council members just so happened to be William Byrd, patriarch of West Hundred, later known as Westover Plantation; another was Benjamin Harrison of Berkeley Plantation.

Other regions throughout Virginia have numerous plantations scattered about, but Ker Place is one of a kind along the marshy coastline known as the Eastern Shore.

Blue Ridge Highlands

When viewed from a distance, the Blue Ridge Mountains truly appear to be blue, the color coming from the isoprene released by the trees. Two major national parks are located here: Shenandoah and Great Smoky Mountains. The area is also home to the famed Blue Ridge Parkway and a portion of the Appalachian Trail. Native Americans made their homes here before the colonists arrived. During the fall and winter months, this part of the state is colder, providing a real sense of how difficult it was for original settlers to survive. Structures that date back to 1800 still exist. Various colleges and universities are located in the area, such as Virginia Tech and Liberty University. Dedicated to agricultural advancement, Virginia Tech is located a short distance from Smithfield Plantation, one of the oldest in the state.

Smithfield Plantation

1000 Smithfield Plantation Road
Blacksburg, VA 24060
(540) 231-3947
www.smithfieldplantation.org

ON THE APPALACHIAN FRONTIER

While the majority of settlers from England, Scotland, and Ireland established the Eastern Shore and coastline of Virginia, a few brave souls headed deeper into her interior—some even farther, into what was called the frontier. Back in the 18th century, before any major land expansion deals, America's lines were still being drawn. Those men and women who decided to forego safety to develop the countryside by their own rules took a major risk. Many did not survive—protection from a militia was virtually nonexistent—but those who did make it were rewarded greatly for their bravery.

James Patton immigrated to the colony in 1740 and was welcomed by William Beverley of Tappahannock. Patton became good friends with the wealthy landowner, who received permission to settle newcomers in and around the Shenandoah Valley. As a ship captain from Ireland, Patton had clout. He chose to bring his family with him, including his sister, Elizabeth; her spouse, John Preston; their son, William; and two of his own offspring.

In 1745 Patton obtained from Beverley the "Great Grant," 100,000 acres along the southwestern part of Virginia. Patton understood that the land needed to be developed and began a land development business soon after. He also was a surveyor, an important occupation for the time, and his surveying skills were closely observed by his nephew. Young William became his uncle's shadow, carefully mimicking and executing business affairs.

During the 18th century, peace agreements had been made with Native Americans in settled eastern areas, but not along the frontier. In 1755 Patton was killed at Draper's Meadows, though his exact burial location is unknown. The night before his uncle's death, William traveled to a neighboring plantation to assist with the harvest. The Shawnees attacked Draper's Meadow the next day, kidnapping Mary Draper Ingles and her children. After being held for seven months, Mary escaped

and walked from what is now Ohio all the way back to Virginia, some 600 miles! Without a male heir, William Preston took control of his uncle's business at the age of 26.

Following in his uncle's footsteps, William became a deputy surveyor in Augusta County, which was established in 1745. Augusta later split into three other counties: Botetourt (1770), Fincastle (1772), and Montgomery (1776). Preston purchased 1,770 acres from John Draper, William Ingles, and Francis Smith. When built in March 1774, Smithfield Plantation occupied Fincastle, but as lines were redefined, the home became a part of Montgomery County, where it remains today. One of Preston's greatest accomplishments was opening up the Kentucky territory to colonists moving westward.

At its height Smithfield Plantation covered some 1,860 acres, occupying land currently known as Blacksburg as well as Virginia Tech. Back then, however, that land was wide open spaces with numerous springs flowing through and around its farmland. This proved vital to the plantation's success.

William Preston married Susanna Smith from Hanover County on July 17, 1761. Before moving into Smithfield, the couple had seven children, then had five more during their time on the plantation. With 12 children running around, the home was probably a busy one. William was not left to engage in farming on his own, as his civic responsibilities reigned supreme. Along with Susanna, slaves were expected to execute the home's daily duties, including caring for and rearing the children.

Preston had five indentured servants and was a slave owner. At any given time he had anywhere between 40 and 90 slaves. According to records, he purchased 18 Africans from Anomabu, West Africa, present-day Ghana. A slave ship named *True Blue* sailed down the Rappahannock River in 1759, delivering this human cargo. There isn't much known about Preston's slaves or how they were treated. What is known is that he respected his overseers, so much so, in fact, that they are buried in the family cemetery. Inside the house, as expected, Preston's slaves did the cooking and other chores. Although a reconstructed slave cabin from one of Preston's other plantations is on-site, this building doesn't resemble the slave quarters that actually existed on the plantation, which have been described as log cabins with dirt floors. Certainly, slavery wasn't an issue for Preston and his contemporaries, but in 80 years, all that would change.

William Preston served in the Virginia House of Burgesses and later as a colonel during the Revolutionary War. During his frequent absences, a militia took up residence in his house to protect his family from Cherokee, Shawnee, and Tories (pre-Revolution). After serving in Williamsburg, he returned to Smithfield influenced by the city's architectural designs.

Boasting spacious rooms and high ceilings, Smithfield was in stark contrast to its neighbors' log cabins. While most Colonial landowners downplayed their wealth, Colonel Preston smacked people in the face with his riches. The L-shaped, timber-framed house is one of the last examples of pre-Revolutionary architecture in western Virginia. The house itself is enormous, consisting of an entrance hall, drawing room, master chamber, and dining room located on the first floor and four rooms on the second.

In the entrance hall hangs a picture of Janie Preston Boulware Lamb, great-great granddaughter of William Preston. Across from her portrait is a Georgian looking glass, original to the house. The yellow Virginia pine floorboards are mostly as they were, with only a few missing. A drawing room opens to the right from the central passage and reveals much about the Preston family, from the piano forte Susanna played to William's library that housed over 270 books. The room's raised panel wainscoting around the mantel hasn't been changed since the house was built.

Across the hallway, the downstairs bedchamber holds two bedsteads. The tradition was that important guests were invited to share sleeping quarters with the husband and wife. A fireplace is painted bright Prussian blue, a very expensive synthetic pigment that was invented in 1705. Subtlety was thrown out the window, as the ability to cover such a large area with a pricey paint certainly shouted wealth.

Straight ahead is the dining room, where three- to five-course meals were served. Slaves transported food up a narrow stairway from a winter kitchen located in the basement. The corner cabinet houses Cantonese export ware, while the display pie safe holds the Staffordshire china.

In the rear, a sizable one-room schoolhouse awaits. Schoolmaster James John Floyd taught the Preston children, including the girls, which was an unusual concept for the 18th century. He later became an employee of Preston's and later married his niece, becoming part of the family. Floyd's son John married the Prestons' daughter Letitia and later served as the governor of Virginia. Subsequently, one of the Prestons' sons, James Patton, who was Smithfield's second owner, would also serve as a Virginia governor from 1816 to 1819.

A white-painted Chinese Chippendale staircase leads upstairs to four bedrooms, but only one is currently opened to the public. Decorated to reflect where children and subsequently grandchildren slept, its cheerful appearance is in contrast to the hard, wooden above-stairs passage where slaves slept on call.

After William's death in 1783 and Susanna's in 1823, Smithfield stayed in the family for 200 years. The last owner was Janie Lamb, who gave the plantation along with 4 acres to the Association for the Preservation of Virginia Antiquities (APVA) in 1959. Previously used to store hay, Smithfield took five years to restore, a project led by a descendant of Thomas Jefferson, Virginia Tech professor George G. Shackelford, and his wife, Grace. It opened to the public in 1965, and 14 years later, in 1979, an additional 7 acres were added. Encompassing 12 acres, the plantation is now completely enclosed by Virginia Tech and has been made into a historic easement. Laid within bricks and a wrought-iron gate, the family cemetery is only a few feet from the house.

To honor the Prestons, their successors created the Smithfield-Preston Foundation to take over the plantation from the APVA. As an independently operated association, the dedication of its members as well as its supporters allows Smithfield to function successfully. Within the home is a museum where artifacts that have been found on the plantation's grounds can be viewed. Each has a story to tell. A team of volunteers keeps the Prestons' legacy alive every day. Known as the Smithfield Patriots, some of the docents have worked at the plantation for over 15 years.

Smithfield remains one of the earliest and westernmost frontier plantations in Virginia. Colonel Preston and his family were pioneers in land development and education for women. Upon his death, he owned over 20,000 acres as well as other plantations, but Smithfield held a special place.

When touring the plantation home today, walk softly and listen to the creak in floorboards that are almost 300 years old, as sunlight pours in from the nine-over-nine paned windows. Be sure to listen closely because in the fall you may hear a cheer or two, as Virginia Tech's football stadium isn't too far away. Here three centuries intertwine with one another—one foot protecting the past, the other forging into the future.

Coastal Virginia— Hampton Roads

The next time you visit the popular tourist attraction of Virginia Beach, think about the first colonists who arrived in 1607, led by Captain Christopher Newport in an event dubbed the "First Landing." Back then the area was called Cape Henry, but today it's known as Hampton Roads, aka Tidewater Virginia. A vacation destination, many people visit Colonial Williamsburg, which is set up as a functioning Colonial town. But that living-history museum is not the only historic attraction worth investigating. Within this geographic triangle there is enough history to keep both experts and the merely curious engaged for long periods of time. Captain Newport didn't stay in Cape Henry. Instead, his group set up Jamestown, the first successful English colony in the New World. That marshy area wasn't idyllic, and most of the settlers became ill and died. Hampton Roads' proximity to the harbor and rivers made it a prime location for commerce and shipbuilding, as well as for numerous military installations, including Old Point Comfort established in 1610 and Gosport Navy Yard in 1767. The area soon became known for its tobacco industry, attracting wealthy landowners who became slave owners. We cover 13 Hampton Roads plantations, many known as the James River Plantations for their location along this beautiful body of water.

Bacon's Castle

465 Bacons Castle Trail
Surry, VA 23883
(757) 357-5976
www.preservationvirginia.org

A HOUSE FIT FOR A KING

Englishman Arthur Allen immigrated to the royal colony in 1649. As a trader, uncharted territories in the New World inspired visions of grandeur for him, as anything was possible. Allen settled in Surry County, founded in 1652, and amassed a substantial amount of wealth and land holdings. Starting out with 200 acres of land, by the 1660s he owned 2,000 acres. The Allens, like many of the new settlers, lived in a smaller house upon their arrival. By 1665 Arthur completed a 9,000-square-foot brick home, known as "Arthur Allen's Brick House."

Styled in the Jacobean fashion, three chimneys enclose each side of the roof that was once English stone shingled. Jacobean architecture reflected the renaissance occurring throughout England, which was shifting slightly from Elizabethan design to one with more foreign influences, ornateness, and curved gables. This curvature can be seen around the stacked chimneys, using Flemish bond for the brickwork.

Born in Surry, Virginia, in 1652, Arthur Allen II (known as Major Allen) was sent to England to be properly educated. In 1669 his father passed away, leaving the plantation to him at age 17. Young Major Allen returned to the rural Virginia colony after getting a taste of English high society.

While in England, young Arthur enjoyed the revival of the "pleasure garden," perfectly man-icured for entertaining, and he decided to re-create something similar at his Surry County home. Wanting to complement the architecture of the existing house, Major Allen oversaw the creation of a garden spanning 1½ acres. In the centuries following its creation, the exact dimensions were lost until the Garden Club of Virginia assisted in excavating the grounds to restore what was assumed to be a 19th-century garden. To their surprise, three centuries' worth of plots were unearthed. Their discovery led to a detailed map of what Arthur Allen II's garden potentially looked like circa 1680.

The garden is now surrounded by a hawthorn hedge on two sides, and pecan, apple, and cedar trees dot the walkway. Other fruits grown included figs, pomegranates, and grapes. Benches have been placed in alcoves that now look out to six rectangular lawns as well as the grounds' holly, ash, willow, oak, and linden trees. In the far corner, the Hankins family cemetery sits next to boxwood. Today this garden is recognized as the oldest English formal garden in North America.

An incident occurring in 1676 gives the plantation its iconic name, Bacon's Castle, named after the events of Bacon's Rebellion. Nathaniel Bacon traveled to the New World in 1673 with hopes of a fresh start, leaving England after his new wife's father strongly voiced his disapproval of their marriage. Bacon united the colonists living on the frontier of Virginia against the perceived injustice of Governor Berkeley's failure to send reinforcements against Indian attacks. This, coupled with low tobacco revenues and a rise in taxes, resulted in an armed rebellion of thousands of men marching to the Colonial capital of Jamestown. Once there, after a confrontation with Berkeley, the rebels set fire to Jamestown, burning it to the ground. Fearing retaliation, Governor Berkeley along with other prominent members of society, including Major Allen, fled to safety along the Eastern Shore.

After the burning of Jamestown, the rebellion broke apart and approximately 80 of the men who followed Bacon took over Major Allen's brick home, eating his food, slaughtering his livestock, and drinking his wine. The encampment ended with the apprehension of the rebels, who were either hanged or sued for damages. In the 1980s an archaeological dig uncovered a trash pit containing numerous animal bones and wine bottles marked with the initials "AA" for Arthur Allen. This find supports the pillaging that occurred until Berkeley's reinforcements arrived. Though Bacon himself never set foot on the grounds, by the 19th century the home was referred to as Bacon's Castle.

Arthur Allen II died in 1710, leaving the plantation to his son, Arthur Allen III, who married Elizabeth Bray. Taking over her husband's affairs, Elizabeth is credited for occupying Bacon's Castle for the longest period of time. She made substantial renovations to the antiquated home built by her grandfather-in-law. Elizabeth entertained many of the landed gentry of the time, and her home reflected a level of grandeur expected in 18th-century Tidewater Virginia. When she died in 1774, she left the house to her grandson, Allen Cocke.

Like the generations before him, Cocke took his civic duties seriously and served in the militia during the American Revolution. After he died in 1794, Bacon's Castle passed between many of his children, finally ending in 1815 with Richard Herbert Cocke. Richard ushered in the 19th century at Bacon's Castle, introducing different types of livestock and adding outbuildings, including an icehouse. Two generations later, his granddaughter, Indiana Allen Henley Robinson, the last descendant of Arthur Allen to live at Bacon's Castle, would mortgage the property. Foreclosed on in 1843, Bacon's Castle was sold outside of the family for the first time.

John Henry Hankins purchased the home in 1845. His wife, Louisiana, grew up near Bacon's Castle. They and their nine children lived alongside 80 slaves, operating a traditional antebellum Virginian plantation. Truly dedicated to its agricultural success, the plantation's self-sufficiency under the Hankins family lasted until the dawn of the Civil War. Architecturally the Hankins made a significant change by adding a neoclassical two-story wing to the east side of the house in 1854, which remains today. After the Civil War, like most Southern planter families, the Hankins were unable to maintain their plantation lifestyle and had to mortgage Bacon's Castle. Within seven years, it was sold.

In 1880 William Allen Warren, who also owned Walnut Valley Plantation, bought Bacon's Castle. Warren rented out farmland to tenant farmers, as he had done with other plantations he owned.

In 1909 he bequeathed Bacon's Castle to his son Charles. A successful businessman, Charles lived in the house until he passed it to his son, Walker Pegram Warren, who with his wife, Violet, used Bacon's Castle as their summer residence. In 1973 the couple died in a car accident and the house along with 40 acres was auctioned to Preservation Virginia.

Preservation Virginia, a nonprofit private organization, was founded in 1889 and cares for some of America's most treasured landmarks, such as Patrick Henry's Scotchtown and Historic Jamestown. For 11 years the organization worked on restoring the home before opening it to the public in 1984. Preservation discussions were intense, and decisions about the authenticity of the site included potentially tearing down its 1854 extension, but the decision was made to properly show each century by embracing the changes over time. In addition, fire doors were added between the 1854 wing in the main house to prevent any damage in case of fire.

Driving down the driveway to Bacon's Castle feels like a movie. The handsome three-story structure with its 19th-century addition does look like a castle. Beginning in the newest part of the house, the 1854 wing holds various rooms as well as the plantation's gift shop. But when those fire doors are opened and you enter a home that recently celebrated its 350th birthday, for a moment you are speechless.

Walking up to the second floor of the original house, you enter an empty bedchamber containing 19th-century graffiti and cutaways to reveal the space's architectural changes over time. Across the hallway, another bedchamber was reconstructed to look as it would have when the 17th-century Allens lived in the home. With modest furniture, a bed draped with yellow fabric gives the dark room a pop of color. Its leaded diamond-shaped panes are re-creations of the original 1665 windows.

In the garret are three smaller rooms facing north, west, and south where, at various times, slaves and indentured servants once slept. Before descending, look up to the ceiling where you can

see exposed beams and nails that have been hammered through the roof. If you're not afraid of heights, look down, as the central stairwell rises the entire height of the house.

The two largest rooms in the house are located on the first floor and reflect the 18th-century changes that occurred during the residency of Elizabeth Bray Allen. The chamber served as Elizabeth's office as well as her bedroom. Scratched into the windowpanes are signatures of the previous residents of Bacon's Castle. Today the room is completely unfurnished with the exception of a few chairs, allowing guests to take in the mid-18th-century woodwork including the mantel and paneling. The hall is furnished to reflect 1755, when Elizabeth Bray Allen's second husband, Arthur Smith, passed away. This room was luxuriously furnished by Elizabeth to entertain and to impress her guests. Fashion plates illustrating the latest clothing designs from Paris hang on the wall, and a fine china tea set is displayed for an afternoon visit.

In the basement is the original kitchen, a rare example of an interior kitchen. In the work yard, many outbuildings remain, including a barn built in 1701 and a smokehouse built in the 1820s. Sniff the air, where a faint scent of smoked meat and rendered fat remains. Next to the smokehouse is an 1829 slave cabin original to the property that was lived in as a tenant house until the 1950s. Upon entering the slave cabin, which is completely intact, you can see how it differed from most slave quarters, as it has a floor. Giving off some type of iridescent glow, perhaps due to the removal of wallpaper and paint, it is a humbling place to stand.

Celebrating its 350th year in 2015, Preservation Virginia launched a campaign called "350 for 350" with hopes to raise $350,000 to continue restoring what is now documented as the oldest brick house in the United States. Tasks such as roof replacement, repointing brick, and improving security will continue to protect this treasured landmark. And if you must take a piece of Bacon's Castle home, check out the re-created wine bottles blown by Jamestown Glasshouse sealed with "AA," just as they were done over three centuries ago. Cheers!

Berkeley Plantation

12602 Harrison Landing Road
Charles City, VA 23030
(804) 829-6018
www.berkeleyplantation.com

PROGRESSIVE BEYOND ITS YEARS

The drive up to Berkeley Plantation is exhilarating, as one passes trees reaching at least 60 feet into the air. A circular driveway allows you to view the home as it has sat since 1726. Hosting the same family until the 19th century, four centuries of history are scattered along terraced grounds that overlook the James River.

Berkeley's initial entry into America's history book came in 1619, long before its home was built. There is some controversy about where the first Thanksgiving was held. Plymouth is regarded as the original location of the notorious feast in 1621; however, Berkeley claims that the iconic American celebration first happened two years earlier on its grounds. When Captain John Woodleaf landed with a handful of other men, they came ashore to give thanks after a harrowing sea journey. It wasn't until the 1960s that historian Arthur Schlesinger Jr., special assistant to John F. Kennedy, acknowledged the distinction, correcting a speech given by the president. That letter, recognizing Berkeley as the site of the first Thanksgiving, now sits in the home's entryway for all to see.

Berkeley Plantation has links to a Founding Father, Benjamin Harrison V, and the ninth president, William Henry Harrison. The first Harrison, Benjamin Harrison, came to America from England in 1630 and landed in Virginia. His son, Benjamin Harrison II, was the father of Benjamin Harrison III, who became a wealthy shipping merchant along the James River. His son, Benjamin Harrison IV, decided to make his own fortune in tobacco and commissioned Berkeley Plantation to be built in 1721.

Upon its completion in 1726, Benjamin IV and his wife, Anne Carter, moved in. Anne was a member of Virginia royalty, as her father was none other than Robert "King" Carter, the largest land holder in Virginia. The couple had 10 children, but tragedy struck early when Mr. Harrison and two of the children died during a storm. It is said Mrs. Harrison died shortly after of a broken heart. Left

with the weight of the world on his shoulders as the eldest son, Benjamin V took over all of Berkeley's responsibilities at the tender age of 19. His leadership continued as he later signed the Declaration of Independence and became the governor of Virginia in 1782. His son William Henry Harrison became the 9th president of the United States, and his grandson Benjamin Harrison became the country's 23rd president.

By 1842 the Harrison family fell onto hard times and abandoned the plantation. Union General George McClellan's 140,000 troops took over its grounds as the Civil War commenced in 1861. Used as a post by the Union until 1865, Berkeley fortunately was not damaged by the surrounding chaos. However, Confederate troops did not hesitate to pester those taking refuge on her massive acreage. General J. E. B Stuart shot cannonballs from over 4 miles away, though many lost their power by the time they reached Berkeley. In 1862 Union Major General Daniel Butterfield, along with brigade bugler Oliver Willcox Norton, created on her lawn what is militarily known as "Taps."

After the Civil War, another occupant came in the unlikeliest form. John Jamieson, a drummer boy for Union troops during the war, had grown into a prominent businessman in New York, making his fortune in the lumber industry. Hearing that the plantation was up for auction in 1907, he remembered the home from his youth and placed what he believed to be a meager bid of $28,000. To his surprise, his bid won. Jamieson sent surveyors to inspect and manage the land. With over 1,000 acres untamed, Berkeley once again began operations.

John's son, Malcom Jamieson, was a bit more curious, wanting to discover more about the plantation. On his way to Charles City, a stop in Richmond led him to meet and marry Grace Eggleston, daughter of a Richmond judge. The newlyweds settled at Berkeley. Decades of dedication have turned Berkeley into what it is today, a tourist destination as well as a National Historic Landmark.

Adjacent to the home sits a "tavern." Information about Berkeley's first Thanksgiving and the Harrison family are on display inside. What is not expected is the large amount of information about the slaves on its grounds, as well as surrounding plantation homes. Refreshing in its approach, binders upon binders await to be leafed through, providing a well-rounded look at plantation life.

At any given time, the Harrison family owned up to 100 enslaved people. Through documentation, names and the price paid for many of the slaves are available to view. Bought in 1781 for 25 pounds of sterling silver, one of the youngest slaves at the tender age of 8 is simply known as

Billy Jones. Twenty-one-year old George Snow commanded 75 pounds, one of the most expensive exchanges on file. Slaves worked tirelessly to fulfill their set quotas of tobacco.

A tunnel built from the kitchen to the main house was recently discovered. Built entirely of brick, the tunnel provided slaves shelter from harsh weather and kept the food from being tepid when it arrived in the dining room. Another way slaves kept food warm was by pouring hot water into a corked serving dish; the steam would warm the serving ware until the food was ready to be eaten. Until the laundry and kitchen are restored to their Colonial makeup, exploration of the tunnel is not allowed.

Currently used as a summer home, Berkeley's second and third floors are still occupied by the Jamieson family, allotting only the first floor to be toured. Nonetheless, those four rooms have welcomed not one, not two, but the first ten US presidents. Berkeley is impressive, as its initial owner could only display his wealth via his house. During Colonial times, talking about wealth was considered crass, so rich landowners found more subtle ways to exhibit their prosperity. And demonstrate is exactly what Benjamin Harrison IV did.

Yet it was a Scottish indentured servant by the name of Robert Wilson who built Berkeley. Harrison paid off Wilson's debts, which had landed him in prison. Wilson was happy to be released and given free passage to Virginia. In exchange for having his debts paid, Wilson was required to build Harrison's home within five years. With the help of enslaved people, Wilson was able to fulfill his obligation within the allotted time. Georgian in style, the three-story brick home is grand. Closely look at its brickwork showcasing various colors, one even noted as purple. A few of the bricks still glisten underneath the sun's rays, providing an indication of Berkeley's glory.

Berkeley's entryway isn't where the awe is evoked, but rather in its sitting room and parlor. Amusingly, Thomas Jefferson once criticized the adjoining rooms known as the north and south parlor, strongly suggesting archways and woodwork to open the space. Harrison obliged. (Friends rarely ignored Jefferson's advice.) Etched into the south parlor's wall is Benjamin Harrison VI's signature. Found by the Jamiesons during renovations in the 1930s, it signifies how strong the Harrison family's presence is woven throughout the house.

Two separate events have prevented Berkeley from owning its original furniture. The first concerns Benedict Arnold, hired by the British to assassinate Benjamin Harrison V, who was alerted

in advance and fled with his family. Arnold, angered that he was not able to carry out the killing, burned all the home's furniture on the front lawn. Returning to an empty house, the Harrisons refurnished Berkeley again, but upon their departure in 1842, vandalizing occurred until Union troops occupied its premises. Whatever was left over was burned for firewood as the war unfolded.

For 289 years Berkeley Plantation has stood the test of time. Standing at her river entrance, manicured gardens stretch down to the James River as native trees enclose graveled pathways, fountains, and planted flowers. Even the willow trees, although not native to Virginia, look as if they belong, with their arched branches sweeping the lawn. This house is a historical treasure and has been since the 1950s thanks to the Jamieson family. Since opening its doors to the public, thousands of tourists have taken a step back in time. When raising your glass for a toast to celebrate the house's 290th year, if it happens to be whiskey you can thank Reverend George Thorpe, who first distilled the spirit in 1622 near Berkeley Plantation along the banks of the James River.

Chippokes Plantation / Jones-Stewart Mansion

695 Chippokes Park Road
Surry, VA 23883
(757) 294-3728
www.chippokes.com

TWO HOUSES FOR THE PRICE OF ONE

Entering a state park, you may not expect to see two historic homes less than a mile apart built within 30 years of each other. Yet when you visit Chippokes Plantation State Park, whether it is for hiking, biking, horseback riding, or the countless other outdoor activities that nature seekers can participate in, there is an additional historical possibility available.

The 1,947-acre park sits across the water from historic Jamestown and is accessible by taking the Jamestown-Scotland Ferry—free to travelers—across the James River. Don't miss the opportunity to get out of your vehicle and head upstairs to one of the waiting areas. Your vantage point may include a trail of seagulls flying close enough to almost touch their wingtips or a bald eagle sitting majestically on buoy #55. Driving off the ferry and down the road to Chippokes, the adventure begins, taking guests back to 1619 when William Powell was granted two land patents, one for 550 acres, the other for 200.

Powell was a representative for James City County (where Jamestown is located) in the Virginia Assembly in 1619 and is believed to have asked for a land grant soon after the assembly's first session. The land given to Powell sat in the heart of territory controlled by the Powhatan Indians, who fiercely fought the invasion of English colonists. In what is known as the Indian Massacre of 1622, Native Americans attacked numerous settlements along the James River, killing a third of the population. Becoming a captain of the local militia, William Powell led an avenging attack in 1623 in which he was probably slain. The origin of Chippokes Plantation's name stems from a secondary

spelling of Chief Chippoke (Chipoaks or Choupocke), a leader under Paramount Chief Powhatan who was friendly toward the English colonists.

Between 1623 and 1678 numerous owners of the property expanded Chippokes Plantation. Governor William Berkeley owned the property on two separate occasions. After he died in 1677, his wife married the prominent Phillip Ludwell I, whose family would go on to own Chippokes from 1678 to 1836. After the American Revolution, the Ludwells appealed to have their land returned to them. Because they were sympathetic to the British, their land was confiscated by the newly established American government. Their friend Thomas Jefferson interceded on their behalf, and their land was returned.

Chippokes was bought in 1837 for $12,000 by Albert Carroll Jones, who is thought to be the first owner to actually live on the property. A wooden structure known as the River House was already present on the property, having been built in 1830. Jones doubled the size of the house to make room for his growing family in 1847. Worked by 13 slaves, his plantation had an abundance of fruit orchards, including apples and peaches. Jones was legally licensed to distill alcohol and made flavored brandies using the fruits from his orchard. He became a wealthy man as his brandy grew popular along the Eastern Seaboard.

In 1844 Jones married Ann M. Baskerville, and two years later they had a daughter named Mary. Tragically Ann passed away in 1850. Jones went on to marry Ann's sister, Roberta, and by 1852 decided to construct another dwelling, this time brick, just southeast of the River House. Referred to as the Jones-Stewart Mansion, it was completed in 1854 using materials from his land.

Folklore has it that the Civil War left Jones's plantation and distilling business untouched due to his providing both sides with alcohol. Though not confirmed, the tale is interesting nonetheless. His daughter and Charles W. Sutton, a veteran of the Confederate army, continued to live in the River House after their marriage. They had a son named Henry. When Albert Jones died in 1881, he left the mansion library, two bedrooms, some furnishings, and one-third of the farm's profits to wife Roberta. Daughter Mary received the rest of the property and its profits. Both Henry and Mary died before Roberta, who willed the property to her relatives in 1910. The plantation, unfortunately, was mishandled and the property was put up for auction in 1918.

Thornton Jefferies and Victor W. Stewart, partners in a lumber company in Petersburg, Virginia, bought Chippokes for $47,000, but by 1925 Victor and his wife, Evelyn, decided to buy out Jefferies for $5,000. Making the plantation their permanent home, the couple began a life committed to agriculture and humanitarianism. Both private college educated—Victor attended Swarthmore and Evelyn graduated from Vassar—the two married in 1909. They were friends with the Rockefellers (who were staunch supporters of historical restoration and funded the development of Colonial Williamsburg), and the couples would visit each other regularly.

Various families lived on the farm and assisted with daily operational tasks, including running a dairy. Today herds of cows roam in fenced areas around the property. Victor was also a conservationist and humanitarian, serving as president of the Virginia Forestry Association in 1943 and later assisting in funding and building the Petersburg Hospital.

Around 1950, modifications were made to the mansion, including the addition of a two-story wing and an adjoining one-story wing that served as a dining room for the farm's tenant employees. An avid equestrian and well-liked woman, it is said on paydays if workers did not come by to pick up their checks, Evelyn would ride around on her horse to deliver them personally. In 1965 Victor passed away in the same hospital that he had helped erect; Evelyn died four years later, leaving the entire estate to the Commonwealth of Virginia as a memorial to her husband. Chippokes Plantation State Park was opened to the public in 1971. Later that same decade, the annual Pine, Pork and Peanut Festival commenced.

Open year-round, the park contains historical structures and archaeological sites dating back to 3,000 BC. Cabins are rented to park guests and are used by volunteers and other groups. A wonderful place to visit, Chippokes is a combination of gorgeous naturalistic views and farming snapshots from the past. And, fortunately, its continuous maintenance by the state will ensure future generations' enjoyment for years to come.

Edgewood Plantation

4800 John Tyler Memorial Highway
Charles City, VA 23030
(804) 829-2962
www.edgewoodplantation.com

A PLACE TO STAY

There are more than 25 plantations situated along the James River. While a handful are privately owned, others no longer exist, with only their foundations and ruins left behind. Those that are open to the public share their history through educational reenactments, historic tours, and social events, but a few tell their stories as visitors enjoy a bit of Southern hospitality. Edgewood Plantation has chosen the latter. Functioning as a bed-and-breakfast, guests have an optimal opportunity to culturally submerse themselves in Edgewood's past.

Operated by Julian A. and Dorothy M. Boulware, the couple bought the mid-19th-century home in 1978. Once a part of "Berkeley Hundred," patented in 1619, the tract later was purchased by Benjamin Harrison. A part of Harrison's land contained a mill built in the early to mid 18th century. Serving as a focal point of the town, the mill provided flour to locals and continued to stand tall during the American Revolution as British troops accompanied by turncoat Benedict Arnold patrolled the area.

Planting an extensive amount of tobacco which over time ruined the soil, Benjamin Harrison V sold off parcels of his land to remain financially sound. One of those tracts was later bought by a miller from New Jersey named Richard S. Rowland. Built in 1854, Edgewood varies from its Georgian and Federal neighbors with its Gothic Revival style, made popular in 1840s and 1850s by Andrew Jackson Downing, a landscape architect. The two-and-a-half-story house and the mill are the last remaining structures on-site.

The house is filled with collectibles, and the Boulwares' antiques are scattered throughout. In the parlor, a black-painted fireplace adorns the elongated room with a Chinese wall matching in color. Ornamental vases line the mantel, sitting across from a wooden sleigh cloaked in purple

velvet. Meals are served at an elegant dining room table, lit by a gold-plated chandelier. The adjoining tearoom has wall-to-ceiling shelves that are lined with old photographs and tea ware.

Two kitchens are located toward the back: one a smaller kitchenette for preparing meals, the other a throwback to the 19th-century, complete with cast-iron skillets hanging above a hearth. A double Country Charm electric oven enclosed by brick and patchwork quilts draped over wooden chairs add to the kitchen's homey feel. From there a set of stairs takes you down to the basement. Take a look at the bar hidden behind wooden beams and under lock and key.

The second floor is accessible by an oval staircase, which leads into a luminous bedroom embellished in creams and pinks. Its most important feature sits in a south-facing window, looking out toward the road. Etched in the bottom left pane is the name Lizzie Rowland. Short for Elizabeth, Lizzie was Richard Rowland's sister. It is said that she died of a broken heart and continues to watch over Edgewood to this day.

With four bedrooms on the second level, two are gorgeously decorated with what appears to be either black walnut or mahogany. Each bed is canopied with white lace, and in one of the rooms, a pair of gloves that are thought to have belonged to General Robert E. Lee make for an interesting piece of Civil War folklore. Edgewood's half-story opens into a large attic room with a secret cubbyhole hiding in the wall. Perhaps once used for storage, the room now holds four beds and is a favorite place for children who visit with their parents. Outside a pool and a moderately sized cottage are present for guests to enjoy, in addition to a man-made waterfall.

Edgewood's 7,000-square-foot mansion may be a place to stay if you are in Charles City, whether it is for an event, touring other plantations, or learning about the mansion's own history. From its American Revolution account to stories from the Civil War, it has a military appeal. Or for those interested in architecture, viewing the Gothic cottage-style home is a treat, as there aren't many like it in the area. If neither of those aspects appeal to your fancy but the paranormal does, when entering the house, do as Mrs. Boulware did upon purchasing the home: Speak kindly to Lizzie, introducing yourself and letting her know you're there to do no harm but to learn and keep Edgewood's legacy alive.

Endview Plantation

362 Yorktown Road
Newport News, VA 23603
(757) 887-1862
www.endview.org

ALL IN THE FAMILY

Roughly 15 years after the 1607 settlement of Jamestown, Thomas Harwood arrived on Virginia's peninsula by boat from England. The Harwoods were an influential and well-connected family in the colonies. Thomas was the nephew of Virginia Company stockholder Sir Edward Harwood, and his brother William was captain-governor of Martin's Hundred settlement on the north shore of the James River, east of Jamestown.

Within a year after his arrival in the colonies, Thomas married a woman named Grace. In 1624 the couple settled on Mulberry Island, located along the James River at the confluence of the War-wick River. Their first son, Thomas Harwood Jr., was born in 1625. The senior Harwood received a 100-acre patent on land near the confluence of the Warwick River and Deep Creek in 1626. Unfor-tunately that land was not farmable, which led the couple to return to Mulberry Island.

Following in the footsteps of his uncle Edward, Thomas Harwood Sr. was elected to Virginia's House of Burgesses in 1629, serving as speaker. Three years later Harwood had increased his land holdings along Skiffes Creek, and by 1635 he had acquired an additional 1,500 acres. He named his plantation Queen's Hith, *hith* meaning river landing or small haven in Old English. In 1642 Queen's Hith was designated as the northern boundary of what was then Warwick County. Upon Thomas Sr.'s death in 1647, his son Thomas Jr. inherited his estate. Following in his father's foot-steps, Thomas Jr. also served in the House of Burgesses, but wasn't able to carry on his father's legacy for long, as he died just five years after him, in 1652.

Thomas Harwood Jr.'s son Humphrey was born in 1649, three years before his father's death. This left Humphrey as the heir to the Harwood fortune, which he inherited upon coming of age. Both his civic and his political career reflected earlier generations of Harwood men, as Humphrey served as a sheriff, a burgess member, and a naval officer. Living until 1698, he increased the Harwood family's acreage to 2,644.

Humphrey's son, Major William Harwood Sr., born in 1676, continued the family's political and social prestige, holding many of the same positions as his forefathers. Tragically, Major Harwood was killed in a riding accident in 1737, bequeathing his oldest son, Humphrey, the family's inheritance. Humphrey's son William oversaw construction of the house now known as Endview Plantation, completed in 1769.

Endview, originally called Harwood's Plantation in addition to Queen's Hith, received its current name, the story goes, because visitors who approached the plantation were greeted first with its side or "end" view. With its Georgian symmetry, the style differed from earlier Colonial-style homes that were usually built in phases resulting in a less-balanced appearance. Considered moderate in size for its era, the 2,350-square-foot two-story house is 62 feet wide by 19 feet deep. In keeping with the Georgian style, Endview has a first-floor central passage with symmetrical exterior doors, allowing air to circulate during the region's stifling summers. Though Endview's builders and masons regrettably are not known, when the property was acquired by the City of Newport News in 1995 and restoration began, 75 to 80 percent of the home remained intact, a testament to the quality of its construction.

Dr. Humphrey Harwood Curtis, great-grandson of William Harwood, acquired the plantation in 1858. He left Warwick County to attend the College of William & Mary and afterward obtained his doctorate degree from Jefferson Medical College in Philadelphia on March 7, 1857. Marrying Maria Whitaker in 1858, he and his wife settled at Endview to start their married lives together. However, four years later the Civil War began. Dr. Curtis answered the call to arms by organizing a volunteer infantry company known as the Warwick Beauregards. Elected captain, Dr. Curtis traded his medical title for one of military significance.

Dr. Curtis served for one year in the Warwick Beauregards. Upon his discharge, he, Maria, and their children relocated to Danville, Virginia, for the rest of the war. Returning in the spring of 1865, the Curtis family came back to find seven African-American families living in their home as well as farming their land. Those families were not trespassers, but placed there by the Freedman's Bureau. Founded in 1865, the Freedman's Bureau's purpose was to help poor whites and freed blacks survive the aftermath of the war. Applying to the federal government for the return of his land, on November 7, 1865, Dr. Curtis's request was granted.

Unlike other planters whose entire financial success depended on their plantations, Dr. Curtis was able to resume his medical profession and continue his livelihood after the war. One of two doctors in Warwick County, his career kept him busy until he died in 1881. Maria outlived her husband by 38 years, residing at Endview until her death in 1919. Though the Curtises' economic standing changed slightly after the war (in 1860 they were listed as the ninth-wealthiest family in the county), their dedication and commitment to their community did not.

Today the historic site consists of approximately 25 acres. Endview's current furnishings mimic those held by the Curtis family and the military officers who occupied the house during the Civil War. One of the two main rooms on the first floor replicates Dr. Curtis's medical office, though it's believed that he had a separate building on the property for this purpose.

Upstairs, a furnished bedroom is across the hall from one containing gear typically used by Confederate and Union soldiers. On the fireplace surround is a message carved by the First New York Mounted Rifles, a Union regiment that occupied the property during the war. An exhibit educates visitors in the basement that once served as the Curtis family's dining room. Before you leave, hike down to the natural spring and stroll along the nature trail.

From the 17th century to the last quarter of the 21st century, members of the Harwood family worked and resided on the same plot of land. Their home was central to their professional and personal lives. Though their name doesn't appear in history books as often as other Virginia families, their story deserves to be told.

Historic Kittiewan

12104 Weyanoke Road
Charles City, VA 23030
(804) 829-2272
www.kittiewanplantation.org

A DIFFERENT PERSPECTIVE

Unlike many other plantations along the James River, Historic Kittiewan documents the evolution of a "middling" 18th-century plantation into a working 20th-century farm. Kittiewan is owned and operated by the Archeological Society of Virginia, which features an archeological focus on the site. The property's location, overlooking Kittiewan Creek and close to the resources provided by the James River, would have been an ideal place for Native Americans to encamp, and artifacts dating back at least 3,000 years have been found on the property.

The Virginia Company gave Captain George Yeardley permission to claim 2,200 acres north of the James River in 1618, including the tract of land that now encompasses Kittiewan, then called Kenwon or Konwon. Yeardley instead claimed land on the south side of the James that later became known as Flowerdew Hundred.

In 1635 Lennon Pierce patented the first parcel of land thought to be the southern portion of the current Kittiewan tract, followed by Rice Hooe and James and John Merryman, who also patented a few hundred acres in the current tract. Charles Roane of Gloucester County patented an additional 450 acres in 1667, incorporating the previously patented lands. The property changed hands numerous times thereafter. Most wealthy planters like Roane did not live on their land; instead, they had tenant farmers or overseers and slaves cultivate their plantations. During the 17th and most of the 18th centuries, tobacco was the principal cash crop.

Built circa 1775, the present manor house at Kittiewan was the home of Dr. William Rickman, who, during his tenure, called his plantation "Milford," possibly after his ancestral home. Dr. Rickman oversaw the operations of Continental army hospitals in Virginia during the Revolutionary War. Rickman married Elizabeth Harrison, daughter of Benjamin Harrison, the owner of Berkeley Plantation

and a signer of the Declaration of Independence. The couple had no children. After Dr. Rickman's death in 1783, Elizabeth married John Edmondson and continued to live in the manor house. In 1790 she and Edmondson sold Kittiewan to Elizabeth's brother, Carter Bassett Harrison, just before she died. William and Elizabeth Harrison Rickman are buried in the family plot at Kittiewan.

The name Kittiewan came to the plantation around 1803, when Collier Harrison, a nephew of Elizabeth Rickman and Carter Harrison, purchased the tract. The land remained under Harrison family control until 1846, when Robert Harrison sold the 1,000-acre property to Dr. William Allen Selden and his wife, the former Jane Douthat. The Seldens, as had the Rickmans and Harrisons before them, operated the property as a farm, using slave labor. Both the US Census and local church records document the presence of slaves at Kittiewan, including several baptisms of enslaved people. The Seldens modified the manor house with a shed-roofed addition on the north side that replaced one of the original rear wings and housed a dining room, kitchen, and central hallway. Interior design elements in the formal paneled rooms were altered, and identical porches were placed at the south and north entrances of the mansion.

The Seldens lived at Kittiewan through the first years of the Civil War, and Jane and her friend and neighbor Julia Tyler, President John Tyler's wife, provided goods and raised funds for Confederate soldiers. By 1863, however, the Seldens may have run into financial difficulty, for they sold the property to four investors, one of whom was William Alexander Stuart, the brother of Confederate General J. E. B. Stuart. Late in the war, Kittiewan and the neighboring properties on the Weyanoke peninsula were temporarily occupied by Union troops while General Grant's forces crossed the James River on their way to Petersburg in 1864. The trenches and gun emplacements that extend across the Kittiewan landscape are the physical reminders of this Civil War action.

For the next 34 years, the farm at Kittiewan was operated by tenant farmers, and the manor house was rented as well. Most notable of the manor tenants was German immigrant Henry Kracke, whose family had arrived in Richmond in 1837. His immediate family, including the Eukers, rented Kittiewan from the late 1870s to the mid-1880s. In 1897 a farmer by the name of William T. Pointer acquired Kittiewan Plantation and moved into the house with his wife, Annie, and their five children. Twelve years later, the Pointers sold the then 525-acre plantation to the Clarks, a couple from Michigan.

When Loren and Nellie Clark arrived at Kittiewan with their baby daughter, Wilma, early in 1910, the manor was in disrepair. The Clark family replastered many of the old walls, but the majority of the house remained untouched. The Clarks farmed the property for the next 40 years. Wilma, who lived at Kittiewan nearly her entire life, became a locally noted musician, piano teacher, and church organist. In 1948 she married William "Bill" Cropper, a native of Maryland's Eastern Shore who had come to Charles City County to visit relatives. The couple electrified the old manor house and began to acquire objects to create a "Museum of Americana."

After Wilma's death in 1985, Bill Cropper continued the couple's mission of preserving Kittiewan Plantation and maintaining its museum. This desire to maintain Kittiewan as a historic site eventually led Cropper to contact the Archeological Society of Virginia (ASV), an organization of which he was a life member. Upon his death in 2005, Bill Cropper left Kittiewan in trust to the ASV.

Today this 720-acre working farm functions primarily to educate guests about Historic Kittiewan, the people who lived and worked there, and the broader history of Charles City County. The visitor center also serves as the ASV headquarters and houses its research library and archeological collections. The manor house and visitor center house artifacts and historic objects owned or collected by Mr. and Mrs. Cropper. Ongoing archeological investigations seek to document both evidence of Native American occupation and the locations of structures that once stood on the property.

Lee Hall Mansion

163 Yorktown Road
Newport News, VA 23603
(757) 888-3371
www.leehall.org

WHAT A DIFFERENCE A WAR MAKES

Richard Decatur Lee (no relation to General Robert E. Lee) inherited land along Skiffes Creek on Virginia's peninsula in the mid-19th century. Due to overplanting of tobacco, the soil on his land was considered poor in nutrition. However, as a young farmer, Richard wasn't afraid to try new techniques and began experimenting to revolutionize his agricultural practices. He used methods now considered commonplace that were innovative in the 19th century, such as rotating crops, the use of fertilizer, and irrigation. In the decade before the Civil War, his land holdings grew considerably.

With his expanding land ownership, Lee increased his wealth significantly in the years before the war. He married his widowed second cousin, Martha Lee Young, in 1844, and the newlywed couple built a home to reflect their social status. With the help of enslaved labor, construction started on the mansion in the mid-1850s and was completed in 1859.

The beautiful Italianate architecture is characterized by brackets under wide eaves and porches topped with decorative railings. Upon completion, the size of Lee Hall Mansion totaled 6,600 square feet and was an impressive centerpiece surrounded by the property's plowed fields. Throughout the house, the Lees decorated to reflect their wealth and influence. In addition to being a planter, Mr. Lee was a magistrate and operated a gristmill.

The home's high ceilings measuring 11½ feet on the first floor and 11 feet on the second floor provided an airiness that can only be truly appreciated during a Virginia summer. Entering the house as the Lees' guests would have, visitors can tour four rooms bisected by a central hall located on the primary floor. On the right, the ladies' parlor is decorated in cream and shades of burgundy, with a Greek Revival wallpaper border lending a distinguished look. It is fairly easy to imagine Mrs. Lee entertaining female guests in this room, especially after an elaborate dinner.

Wanting to follow current design trends for upper-class residences, Mr. Lee included two parlor rooms in his home, one for the ladies and one for the gentlemen. The sliding pocket doors at the rear of the ladies' parlor open into a masculine salon. A round table that once belonged to Confederate General A. P. Hill is cloaked by a tablecloth and covered with papers and writing tools, as this room would later become an epicenter for the Confederate army.

The music room across the hallway represented Mrs. Lee's upper-class position, as women of her status were expected to know how to play some type of musical instrument for entertainment and to attract the attention of a possible suitor. The piano now in the music room belonged to Martha Lee's first husband's brother, William Young, of nearby Denbigh Plantation.

Naturally the dining room sits beside the room where guests were entertained. Used for more formal dinners that involved numerous courses, the elongated table accommodated the Lees' guests who came to dine and visit. Upstairs, two bedrooms and a more informal sitting room are currently on the tour. Mrs. Lee had two boys from her previous marriage and seven children with Mr. Lee, though only four of the children survived into adulthood.

Two teenage half-sisters of Mrs. Lee, Laura and Angie, lived with the Lees as well. One of the bedrooms is interpreted as their room, though it pales in comparison to the master bedroom across the hall. Walking in even on an overcast day, the light is angelic. Windows look out as far as the eye can see, with a picture of George Washington hanging above the fireplace and a crib at the foot of the bed. In the corner, a comfortable chair with a throw seems like the perfect place for someone to read on a rainy day. The room has a lived-in feel, as if the Lees had just stepped out on an errand.

Only two years after moving into their new home, the Civil War broke out. In spring of 1862, the Lee family left the residence, not to return until the war was over. Taking along some furnishings and most of their slaves, the Lees settled on the outskirts of Richmond, then finally Danville, Virginia. Confederate General John Bankhead Magruder occupied the mansion for use as his headquarters. Heavy fighting rapidly ensued on the peninsula, and on May 4, 1862, a skirmish was fought on Lee Hall's property.

Returning to Lee Hall after the war, the Lees came back to nothing. Due to the outcome of the war, Richard Lee had to appeal to the federal government for the return of his property. Even with its return, enslaved labor no longer provided the foundation needed to support agricultural success. This would lead him to be greatly in debt by 1870, having to declare bankruptcy later that year. In 1871 the house was sold.

Ownership of the house and adjacent property was transferred several times until the City of Newport News purchased the house along with 15 acres of land in 1996. After renovations to the house totaling $2.5 million, Lee Hall Mansion opened to the public on September 19, 1998. It is the sole surviving antebellum Italianate Greek Revival manor located on the lower Virginia peninsula.

Piney Grove at Southall's Plantation

16920 Southall Plantation Lane
Charles City, VA 23860
(804) 829-2480
www.pineygrove.com

HISTORIC HOMES' FINAL RESTING PLACE

Traveling along a curved, rural road, don't blink or you may miss Piney Grove at Southall's Plantation tucked away behind dogwood trees. The property has become a safe haven for historic homes that are either facing hardships or have been selected for demolition. Whether considered an architectural passion or a blessing in disguise, three houses now call the 7-acre property home: Piney Grove, the owners' personal residence; Ladysmith; and Ashland are located just a stone's throw from one another, making it extremely easy to hopscotch among them. This story focuses only on Piney Grove, however, as it is one of the oldest and best-preserved log structures in Virginia.

One of the initial eight counties of Virginia, Charles City County sits between the James and Chickahominy Rivers, the latter named for the Chickahominy tribe that resided in the area during John Smith's expedition. It was here that the Southall family chose to settle in the 1700s. Furneau Southall farmed the 300-acre plot and raised livestock. Worked by slaves, the plantation also had a mill which is no longer standing.

Considered upper middle class, Mr. Southall was a tier below more prominent planter families such as the Byrds, Carters, and Harrisons. However, he was not poor by any means, as he owned slaves to assist in the daily execution of the plantation. The slaves' names appear in tax records and in mortgage records at the courthouse. The original plantation house is no longer standing, thought to be completely dismantled in the 1850s. The log cabin that visitors currently tour was previously used as a corn crib for Southall's cows.

Southall served as a captain in the Revolutionary War under Benjamin Harrison V and was among the Committee of Safety along with Otway Byrd, son of Colonel William Byrd III. Dying in 1790, Captain Southall unwisely did not leave a will, and for the next several decades his family squabbled over his estate. Unable to come to an agreement, the estate went up for auction. Southall descendant Melville Vaiden bought Piney Grove in 1848, and John S. Stubblefield bought it from him in 1850.

By 1857 Edmund A. Saunders bought the property from Stubblefield, naming it Piney Grove after his childhood home. Saunders served in the commissary of the Confederate army and later moved to Richmond. Going into business with Alexander Walker, the two started a wholesale grocery called Walker & Saunders. The firm evolved to E.A. Saunders and then to E.A. Saunders and Sons. Moving from his modest home to Richmond, Saunders lived in a 6,000-square-foot home and later a 10,000-square-foot mansion.

In 1874 Saunders sold Piney Grove to Thomas F. Harwood, a former color sergeant in the Confederate army who lost his leg while fighting in the Battle of Malvern Hill. He was treated by Captain Sally Tompkins, the only female commissioned during the war. He also met James Edward Hanger, who began making prosthetics for injured soldiers. Harwood's leg was one of the first prototypes of Hanger Prosthetics and Orthotics, today known as Hanger Inc. and one of the largest prosthetic companies in the world.

In 1917 Piney Grove was purchased by John A. Hughes, who lived there for six years. His son took over the property in 1916 and owned it until 1964. For the next 20 years, the house remained abandoned. When Joseph and Joan Gordineer came across Piney Grove, their intention was to make the property home. However, much work needed to be done, as the roof was gone. Joseph and Joan and their family have lived here ever since, and they continue to give tours to interested passersby. Although many modifications were made in the 19th and 20th centuries, that exquisite pre-1790 log cabin still stands.

Sherwood Forest Plantation

14501 John Tyler Memorial Highway
Charles City, VA 23030
(804) 829-5377
www.sherwoodforest.org

THE HOME OF "AMERICA'S ROBIN HOOD"

President John Tyler was born on March 29, 1790, in Charles City County, Virginia, the sixth of Judge John Tyler and Mary Armistead Tyler's eight children. John's mother died when he was only 7 years old; however, his father continued to guide his children with a loving hand. Judge Tyler had been friends and roommates with Thomas Jefferson, which contributed to his Republican ideology, which he passed on to young John. Graduating from the College of William & Mary at the age of 17 in 1807, Tyler was elected to the Virginia House of Delegates four years later. He married Letitia Christian, the daughter of another prominent planter in the area, on March 29, 1813. Marrying into another affluent family assisted in Tyler's political and social ascension.

The young couple built a plantation called Woodbourne close to Greenway, John's childhood home. When he was elected to the United States House of Representatives in 1816, Letitia stayed behind to manage their home. Retiring from Congress on January 15, 1821, due to a digestive disorder contracted in the federal city, Tyler came home to his wife and three children. He would go on to father 12 more children for a total of 15, the most of any US president.

Tyler returned to Washington in 1826 as a senator. It was a tumultuous time, as President Andrew Jackson came into power and began implementing various tariff acts passed by Congress between 1828 and 1832. As tensions ran high, Jackson was succeeded by vice president Martin Van Buren, who later was replaced by William Henry Harrison with Tyler as his vice president. Harrison died on Sunday, April 4, 1841, the first president to die in office. Two days later, John Tyler was sworn in as the 10th president of the United States. A year into his presidency, Letitia died on September 10, 1842; her body was returned to Virginia to be buried in her family cemetery. During this time President Tyler purchased a 1,600-acre plantation called Walnut Grove in Virginia, close

to Woodbourne and Greenway. In 1843 he renamed it Sherwood Forest, picturing himself as a latter-day American Robin Hood.

In 1843, during his presidency, John met Julia, the daughter of New York Senator David Gardiner, at a social gathering she was attending with her sister Margaret. Though 30 years her senior, President Tyler was attracted to Julia. He first asked the young woman to marry him on February 22, George Washington's birthday, but Julia turned him down. Not to be dissuaded, President Tyler bided his time.

Tragedy struck one year later during a party aboard the USS *Princeton*, a naval ship. The highlight of the night would be the firing of the "Peacemaker," considered the world's largest naval gun. Fired twice, the gun delighted the guests in attendance on the ship, which included Julia, Margaret, Senator Gardiner, and President Tyler. But upon passing Mount Vernon, someone a suggested that the naval gun should be fired once again in honor of George Washington. The gun malfunctioned, hitting many who had gathered on deck to watch the display. Those that had gone below to enjoy the festivities were lucky, as many above deck lost their lives, including Julia's father. Hearing the tragic news, Julia fainted and President Tyler tended to her. Perhaps due to her grief, shortly after Julia decided to marry him.

President Tyler served only one term, and he and Julia returned to Sherwood Forest, which became the longest symmetrically framed dwelling in America due to a colonnade and a 68-foot-long ballroom added circa 1844–1845. There the couple would often invite their guests to dance. From a president to a planter, Tyler managed the cultivation of grain on his plantation. Meanwhile, the topic of slavery continued to be debated throughout the country and the world.

Although Julia had been born in New York, the fruits of slave labor had benefited her as well. A little novel by the name of *Uncle Tom's Cabin* caught the eye of abolitionists and supporters alike, and as tensions grew, Julia defended her position on slavery in the 1853 issue of *Southern Literary Messenger*. Soon, the world was watching, and on March 6, 1857, the Supreme Court in the Dred Scott decision ruled that slaves were not to be considered citizens. Things continued to go south, and on December 20, 1860, South Carolina would be the first state to secede from the Union. Other Southern states would soon follow. A slave owner himself, Tyler wanted to see the country come together, and on February 5, 1861, was elected president of a peace conference between the states. Unfortunately, an agreement was not to occur, and within two months the Civil War began. Tyler would not see the outcome of the war, dying on January 18, 1862.

Julia and her children moved to Staten Island, New York, to escape the war, and she did not return to the area until 1871. President Tyler was not recognized by the Union, as he was considered a Confederate supporter. However, in 1915 Congress finally did note his contributions by building a monumental 20-foot-tall marble shaft at the cemetery where he and Julia are buried.

Sherwood Forest plantation remained in the Tyler family, and in the 1970s John Tyler's grandson, Harrison Ruffin Tyler, and his wife, Payne Bouknight Tyler, began restoring the mansion. Located on Route 5 where plantations such as Westover, Berkeley, and Shirley also stand, the road is now called the John Tyler Memorial Highway.

Sitting a half mile or so from the road, Sherwood isn't visible even from the parking lot; however, the elongated house is a sight to behold. The 25-acre grounds and mansion are beautifully situated among a variety of 80 species of trees, some from President Tyler's tenure. With its Greek Revival architecture, added by John and Julia during their residency, Sherwood has changed drastically since its 17th-century construction. The first house built no longer stands, but by 1720 a second house of Georgian style was erected along with separate outbuildings. With the addition of a wing, the main house was soon connected to some of its dependencies around 1780. The connecting of its laundry and kitchen was a modern touch that set it apart from other Tidewater plantations.

The central passage is lined with portraits, including those of President Tyler and Julia. Oriental rugs are laid out in a cross-like pattern, contrasting the cream-colored walls and floral-patterned furniture. The formal dining room is brightly lit by sunlight and a hanging crystal chandelier. Its folding dining table seats a party of six, while a smaller table seats four additional people. Attractive pieces of polished silver illustrate the class and wealth of the Tyler family. Payne Tyler, wife of John Tyler's grandson, wrote a book titled the *James River Plantations' Cookbook: A Glimpse into the Homes and Kitchens of Old Virginia*. Paying homage to days gone by as well as honoring many of the Charles City plantations that share Sherwood Forest's colonial history, the book highlights homes that are now either publicly or privately owned. From Carter's Grove, which was privately bought for the handsome sum of $20 million, to North Bend, which now operates as a bed-and-breakfast, it is a fascinating look at America's culinary history. A few recipes have our mouths watering, like Sherwood Forest's baked Virginia ham, Berkeley's pecan pie, and Tyler's mint julep.

Down the hallway, a masculine room with marble statues, dark wood furniture, musical instruments, and oil paintings looks like the perfect place to relax after a grand meal in the dining room. But if sitting doesn't appeal to your tastes, farther down the hallway is that 68-foot-long ballroom that President Tyler added almost 200 years ago. With its light green curtains and matching border paper, it is one of the best rooms in the house. One can almost hear the lively music and laughter that look place within these walls. Ten chairs, five on each side, patiently waited for exhausted dancers to sit and rest.

There is talk of paranormal activity in the house, and although the second floor is unavailable to tour, a docent will make sure that you see a spot on the wall that is said to resemble the "Gray Lady." Her spirit, though friendly, is thought to haunt Sherwood Forest, and sometimes when all is quiet in the mansion, you can hear her footsteps going up and down the hidden staircase where her impression is found.

As a US representative, senator, vice president, and president, John Tyler made

significant political contributions to America during the early and mid 19th century. However, his love for his family was just as powerful. Nowhere is this more evident than in the home he built with Julia. Considering himself an outlaw politically, his Sherwood Forest is far from a rogue plantation, but rather embodies his calm demeanor and levelheadedness. A rare beauty indeed.

Shirley Plantation

501 Shirley Plantation Road
Charles City, VA 23030
(804) 829-5121
www.shirleyplantation.com

VIRGINIA'S OLDEST PLANTATION

Considered the oldest active plantation as well as the oldest family-owned business in Virginia, Shirley Plantation continues to operate into the 21st century. With unobstructed views of the James River and plots of crops dotting the landscape, it is hard to imagine that this stately house has been in the same family for over 11 generations.

Starting out as part of a 4,000-acre gift granted to Sir Thomas West for his previous service as governor to Jamestown, the acreage was named "West and Sherley Hundred." A hundred was the number of people desired to settle an area to protect one another from the rugged terrain and threats posted to early settlers. West had very poor health while at the colony and returned to England in 1611, but died during a return trip to Virginia in 1618. His wife, Lady Cessalye Sherley, for whom the Sherley Hundred was named, promptly sold her shares of the land. Ownership changed hands numerous times until 1638, when Captain Edward Hill and his wife, Hannah Aston, registered almost 3,000 acres in county records. It is here that Shirley Plantation's history begins. Although the original home that housed the first three generations of the Hill family no longer exists, archaeological excavations have placed it not too far from the house that stands today.

When Elizabeth Hill, youngest daughter of Edward Hill III, inherited all of Shirley Plantation upon his death in 1726, she became a highly desirable bachelorette. Unfazed by the many men who pursued her, it was John Carter, son of Robert "King" Carter, who finally won her heart. Their engagement solidified the two families' lineage as part of Virginia royalty. John and Elizabeth built the mansion we know today; however, its construction took over 15 years, an unthinkable amount of time even by today's standards.

The four-story building, which includes a basement, demanded a large labor force, mostly composed of slaves. This was not an issue for the Carter family, as "King" Carter is said to have owned over 1,000 slaves of his own. However, by the time the Carters moved into what they called the Great House, they were only able to enjoy it as a family of six until 1742, when John Carter succumbed to dropsy. Son Charles Carter inherited Shirley, although Elizabeth lived there until 1771. From Charles on, the house continued to remain under family control, later owned by Dr. Robert Carter (1771–1804), Hill Carter (1796–1875), Robert Randolph Carter (1825–1888), and Alice and Marion Carter, sisters who bore no male heirs to inherit Shirley.

Alice Carter, like her father, had a knack for farming and took kindly to the plantation. She entertained guests such as Theodore Roosevelt and John D. Rockefeller and did so until her death in 1926. Her sister was left to manage the home, but Marion, who was 70 at the time, didn't have the energy to keep up the plantation on her own, so she called in her cousin Charles Hill Carter Jr. (1919–2009). A tenth-generation Carter, Charles had been helping around the farm since he was a young boy. He inherited the home upon Marion's death in 1952 and proceeded to open Shirley's doors to the public. From that time forward, Shirley's nearly 400-year history has captured all that walked through her doors.

Militarily the plantation saw just as much action, commencing with Edward Hill II's supposed involvement in Bacon's Rebellion, of which he was later cleared. Charles Carter provided livestock to the Continental army and allowed Shirley to serve as a supply depot and listening post for Lafayette's troops. Hill Carter, grandson of Charles, served in the War of 1812 as a midshipman, showing ferocious bravery during the Battle of Cape Canaveral at the tender age of 16. Because of this, he was awarded a congressional sword, which left the home's confines in 1882 to be housed by the Virginia Historical Society. In 2008, 126 years later, the sword was returned to its rightful place and now sits in the home's dining room.

It was in the years leading up to the Civil War that various Carter men showed courage and loyalty to Virginia, including their famously recognized cousin, Robert E. Lee. Choosing between the nation and their beloved state proved to be challenging. States such as Alabama, Georgia, Mississippi, and Tennessee had already seceded by the time Virginia did on April 4, 1861, and it wasn't long before Hill Carter enlisted to fight. No longer a spry 16-year-old, at the age of 65 he brought along his six sons who held positions in sectors ranging from artillery and infantry to cavalry and navy.

However, it was the women of these men who were truly heroic. Robert Randolph Carter's wife, Carter, Louise Humphreys Carter, awoke one morning to a lawn full of wounded Union battalions. Though leery, she and the plantation's other women displayed Southern hospitality at its finest, tending to the soldiers' injuries and providing other provisions. When Hill Carter returned he politely but forcefully wrote a letter to Major General G. B. McClellan about the plantation's losses, and in return the general not only thanked his family for their service to the enemy but issued a federal safeguard. The document protected the Carter family, Shirley Plantation, and its surrounding grounds from any Union military action. With Union soldiers posted at Shirley's gates, anyone who dared to defy the order would suffer the consequences, including possible death.

Robert Randolph Carter felt a duty to serve his country and joined the United States Navy at age 16, just as his father had almost 30 years earlier. In 1861 he left to serve the Confederate navy and from there worked alongside some of the top-ranking officials in the Confederacy, such as President Jefferson Davis and General Stonewall Jackson. General Robert E. Lee had fond memories of Shirley, as his mother, Ann Hill Carter Lee, was married in the parlor to General Henry "Harry" Lee back in 1793, and he had also often played with his cousins in the picturesque countryside. In letters to Hill Carter, he expressed his sorrow at not being able to stop at Shirley during his frequent marches around Virginia.

Slavery was the crux of the war, as Southern states had maintained a certain way of life since Colonial times. Slaves were an important part of the Carters' livelihood. Out of the 785 slaves owned by Charles Carter, it is said that anywhere from 80 to 290 worked Shirley at any given point in time, although that number dropped drastically as agricultural became modernized. One of the earliest records on file is of Joe Mason, age 24, a slave owned by Charles Carter in 1783, while one of the last was Harry Washington, a boy of 15 who ran away to join the Union gunboats in 1863. Before Hill Carter, the staple crop was tobacco, but as other plantations had experienced, Shirley's soil depleted quickly. Hill decided to change the crops to wheat and corn, shifting the plantation's dependence away from tobacco. This created an effective supply-and-demand environment, as his neighbors still heavily harvested tobacco.

Hill's father, Dr. Robert Carter, had viewed slavery as an immoral practice and pursued a career in medicine. Heeding his father's advice, Hill approached slavery in a practical manner and supplied his slaves with satisfactory housing, two outfits for both summer and winter seasons, and regular doctor visits. Families were seldom split apart while working on Shirley, a rarity for the times. Slaves that worked the fields lived in wooden cabins called great quarters, none which are present today. Built in a single row of 15, two families lived in each of the cabins that sat about a mile from the house. Only one cabin remains today, constructed around the 1840s. Its survival is due to the fact a family resided there long after the end of slavery.

Guests who visited the Carters were in awe of their prosperity, and no more was this evident than the layout of the plantation. Because visitors arrived by either land or water, there wasn't a designated entrance to the home; however, those who arrived by river were greeted by the family's carriage, which carried them to the land-facing entrance where they entered the Great Hall. For those who entered from the terrestrial side, their eyes roamed to see what is known as a Queen Anne forecourt, the only example in the United States. On-site there was a laundry, pump house, icehouse, store-house, kitchen, smokehouse, stables, dovecote, and two flanker buildings, all made of brick.

The original pump house built in 1771 no longer exists. It supplied water to other buildings like the kitchen and, of course, the Great House, in addition to the trough for the farm animals. The

two-story kitchen continuously operated, as the Carters entertained frequently. Shirley's advanced technology included the kitchen, where in 1834 Hill Carter placed a "rotary" cooking stove, the 19th century's latest culinary invention.

Three buildings in particular hold significant architectural importance: the icehouse, the dovecote, and the smokehouse. With no refrigeration, having an icehouse was a symbol of status. Blocks of ice were formed from Shirley's freshwater ponds and carried to the L-shaped, 25-foot-deep ice pit. Hill Carter recorded 20 tons of ice being housed at any given time around 1823. Shirley's dovecote sheltered young pigeons, known as squab, until the late 1940s. The smokehouse was in use until 1953. Using green wood and other materials, salted meat was smoked to preserve it.

A constant influx of guests stayed in the north and south flankers. Both structures stood three stories tall and measured 60 by 24 feet. One was destroyed by lightning and the other dismantled for its materials. Today only a root cellar remains where its predecessor, the northern flanker, once sat.

By the time visitors entered the Great House, they may have already been overwhelmed, but the grounds were merely a taste of what was to come. Guests would immediately be greeted by a flying staircase that reached from the first floor to the third, its floating appearance having no outwardly visible support. Later in the 1970s, the Carters discovered it was held up by two 2-inch-wide, ½-inch-thick iron straps hammered into a 12-inch wooden beam that spans the entire width of the house.

Portraits hang along the wall, including Robert "King" Carter as well as Elizabeth Hill and John Carter. Beautiful, original Virginia yellow pine floors stretch throughout the house, creaking slightly under the weight of each footstep. The sitting parlor holds various pieces of the family's furniture, ranging from 1740 to the present. Hand-carved woodwork along with painted wood paneling encase the room, yet it is the two brass faucets that are worthy of attention. Also serving as a dining room at times, its brass faucets delivered hot and cold water to rinse the countless dishes being used at any given time. Guests left the Carters' home with an absolute sense of awe.

It may be unimaginable that the now 700-acre Shirley is still in use, but the family business is alive and well. The same tenant family has tended to the soil for the last 40 years and the farm still grows wheat and corn, along with cotton and soybeans. Currently the 11th generation of Carters call Shirley home, with Charles Hill Carter III serving as the plantation's executive director and his brother Robert Randolph Carter holding the title of deputy director. In the years to come Shirley's story will continue to be told by future generations, as the Carter family was excitedly awaiting the arrival of the 12th generation in 2016.

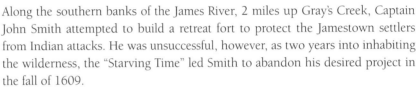

Smith's Fort Plantation

217 Smith Fort Lane
Surry, VA 23883
(757) 294-3872
www.preservationvirginia.org

"A MEMORY STAINED IN TIME"

Along the southern banks of the James River, 2 miles up Gray's Creek, Captain John Smith attempted to build a retreat fort to protect the Jamestown settlers from Indian attacks. He was unsuccessful, however, as two years into inhabiting the wilderness, the "Starving Time" led Smith to abandon his desired project in the fall of 1609.

Another settler, John Rolfe, came to Virginia and was one of the first to become wealthy in the tobacco industry. He also served as secretary of the colony. After the English captured Pocahontas, Rolfe came to know and fall in love with her at the English settlement called "Bermuda Hundred." Following their marriage, the couple received land from her father, Chief Powhatan, which contained Captain Smith's earlier fort site. In 1615 Pocahontas gave birth to their only child, Thomas Pepsironemeh Rolfe. John and Pocahontas did not live on the land given to them by her father, and when Thomas was a year and a half, the family traveled to England, where they were warmly welcomed. In 1622 Pocahontas fell ill with what was thought to be tuberculosis and died at the age of 22.

Leaving Thomas in the care of his brother Henry, John returned to Virginia, remarried, and had other children. But he was only to endure the hardships of Virginia for five more years before he passed away in 1622. Back in England, Thomas was being suitably cultivated by English society and did not return to Virginia until 1635, when he was 20 years old. Like his father, Thomas farmed

tobacco and engaged in various civic duties, making a name for himself throughout the colony, but he never resided on his inherited property. Thomas's absence from Virginia for 13 years had allowed others to settle on the property, but without patents. After a marriage producing no sons, by 1650 he sold the property to Thomas Warren, who in 1652 built a 50-foot brick house on the land.

Sometime in the mid-1750s, following a long and complex series of owners, Nicholas Faulcon bought the acreage and built a house, which is present today, for his son Jacob Faulcon. Jacob was a tobacco planter and slave owner, and ran his own shipping company in the port town of Cobham at the mouth of Gray's Creek nearby.

In 1928 John D. Rockefeller Jr. purchased the property through the Williamsburg Holding Company and began restoration of the house, which had fallen into disrepair. The Rockefellers were also instrumental in the restoration of Colonial Williamsburg. Several years later, in 1933, the Manor House and 27 acres were sold to the Association for the Preservation of Virginia Antiquities (APVA)

for one dollar. The following year the organization began its own renovations with the assistance of the Thomas Rolfe Branch of the APVA and the Garden Club of Virginia.

With its English and Flemish bond exterior brick, the one-and-a-half-story house has a remarkable story about a visit from descendants of its last private owners. One day when site coordinator Tom Forehand was working, a large family arrived in a few cars, contemplating whether to take a tour. Tom, sensing their hesitance, offered some information. One of the women asked, "Is that butter stain still on the cupboard shelf?" It was her grandmother who had made the mark years before with a butter press. During restoration, no matter how many layers of paint were attempted, the stain remained. Tom confirmed her "insider" question and took the entire group on a tour of the house that had once been in their family.

Smith's Fort Plantation's connection to John Smith, Pocahontas, John Rolfe, and other important figures in American history is astounding. Whether seeing Smith's work at the creek, the manor house itself, or the manicured gardens, Smith's Fort is not to be missed.

Walnut Valley Plantation

State Route 634
Highgate, VA 23883

OFF THE BEATEN PATH

What makes Walnut Valley so special is that it's a bit off the radar. Located in Surry County (famous for their country hams), the plantation is off the beaten path and hasn't quite yet opened its doors to the public, but it will. Its initial owner, William Newsum, obtained the 550-acre tract in 1636. The succession of proprietors following Newsum is difficult to trace, but some possible owners include William Batt and Ralph Jones. Throughout the 18th century, members of the Jones family, including James and William, owned Walnut Valley. The Joneses built the plantation house in 1770.

William C. Jones, son of Richard Jones, acquired the property around 1806. William was considered a prosperous man by census documentation and owned about 20 or so slaves. Much of his wealth didn't come from his acreage nor his materialistic possessions, but from his slaves. Skilled males were the most valuable, followed by a woman with child. Some slaves commanded upward of $1,000 but over time their price diminished, and they actually became a burden when they couldn't work to offset their upkeep.

How William treated his slaves is unknown, but an indication might be in how their dwellings were constructed. Built in 1816, an original slave cabin can be found a couple of feet from the house. Its tattered wood is deceiving, as a structural investigation conducted by the National Register of Historic Places revealed that parts of the cabin were built with brick. Furthermore, a floor is thought to have once been present, an upgrade from the usual slave condition of sleeping on a cold dirt floor. The undisturbed cabin still stands, awaiting its restoration.

The one-and-a-half-story home doesn't shy away from the spotlight either, but there is much work to be done. Whether it's replacing the English and Flemish bond brickwork, taking a paint analysis to complete the walls and ceilings, or simply refurbishing its interior to reflect various owners and time periods, Walnut Valley is patient.

In William C. Jones's will, he bequeathed Walnut Valley to his son Bolling (Bowling) Green Jones. Receiving the property in 1834, he lived there until his death. However, without a clear will, the Joneses couldn't agree on how to divide his assets. Blair Pegram, the husband of Bolling's niece Minerva, purchased the plantation from the family in 1858. Almost 60 years later, Minerva in her will bestowed life rights to the house and land to her daughters. A son of one of the daughters, Walker Pegram Warren, had taken ownership of Walnut Valley by 1920.

Financial support came from tenant farming. The Warrens started leasing Walnut Valley to the Mitchells in the 1920s, who farmed the land for years. Raymond Holt Mitchell, who is now in his 80s, still farms the land today. Sadly, in 1973 Mr. and Mrs. Warren died in a car accident without any heirs. Their estate, managed by close friends, allowed a real estate developer to run their own company, Reasor Corporation, on-site. Upon the developer's death in 1999, Lucy Reasor gave Walnut Valley to the Department of Conservation, which later transferred it to the state park in 2004.

As the site is cleaned of debris and a plan is developed to restore Walnut Valley to its past appearance, there are lofty aspirations for the property's future.

Westover Plantation

7000 Westover Road
Charles City, VA 23030
(804) 829-2882
www.westover-plantation.com

COLONIAL ARCHITECTURE AT ITS FINEST

A part of the James River Plantations, Westover is as beautiful as text and portraits originally painted it. Overlooking the James River, it sits 150 feet off the embankment, in close proximity to the other grand homes that reside along the waterfront. Built in the 18th century, the home was one of the "hundreds" granted by the King of England. "Hundreds" referred to the number of people desired to settle an area to protect one another from the rugged terrain and threats posed to early settlers. As Jamestown was being settled farther east, these plots of land were for those looking to have a fresh start of their own.

Written about as early as 1616 by John Rolfe, husband of Pocahontas, it is thought that West Hundred was named for Francis, Nathaniel, and John West, younger brothers of Thomas West, also known as Lord Delaware, who held the prestigious title as the first governor of Colonial Virginia. In 1637, 2,000 acres were patented to Captain Thomas Pawlett. Seven years later, Captain Pawlett died, leaving the land to his brother Sir John Pawlett, who lived in England. In 1665 the plot was sold to Theodorick Bland, a Speaker of the House of Burgesses. Westover stayed in the Bland family until 1688, when it was purchased by William Byrd I. Son of a prominent goldsmith, Byrd continued to build his familial wealth.

His son, William Byrd II, was born in 1674 and left for England at the age of 7. He returned after his father's death in 1704 to take care of the estate. Having lived in England most of his young adult life, Byrd II traveled back and forth between London and the undeveloped colony. A member of the House of Burgesses and King's Council, a surveyor, and a planter, Byrd kept detailed records, consisting of letters as well as his personal diaries. A first edition titled *The Secret Diary of William Byrd II of Virginia, 1709–1712* wasn't published until 1940. In it, everyday life is discussed, ranging from what he ate for the day to treatment of his slaves.

William Byrd II inherited more than 200 slaves from his father and remained active in Virginia's growing slave trade. One slave in particular, Jenny, was often subjected to his and his wife's anger. Numerous entries in Byrd's diary mention whippings and even burning a slave with an iron. While slaves were regarded as property, it seems that Byrd's cruelty was not without remorse. A few of his diary entries asked God's forgiveness for being extremely cruel in punishing slaves.

Tobacco was Westover's dominant cash crop, although it was not solely relied upon to maintain the family's wealth. Byrd II had other business ventures and is credited with founding the prosperous city of Richmond. He died in 1744, bequeathing everything to his son William Byrd III. Tens of thousands of acres now were in Byrd III's possession, making him an eligible bachelor and attracting the attention of Elizabeth Hill Carter, granddaughter of Robert "King" Carter. The couple married in 1748.

William Byrd III had a half-sister from his father's first marriage named Evelyn. Falling in love with someone their father disapproved of, she is said to have died from a broken heart. She was friends with Anne Harrison of Berkeley Plantation, and the two are said to have made a promise that whoever died first would come back and visit the other in good faith. It is said that sometimes Evelyn returns to Westover, but always in a happy manner.

At some point West Hundred's name became Westover, and it has remained as such ever since. Previously, William Byrd II was credited with building Westover's home; however, after further examination of wood rings, the house probably was constructed during his son's time, around 1750 or so. Thought to be one of the greatest examples of Georgian architecture in America, its main building is three stories high, while hyphens connect a west and east wing. Symmetry, a characteristic of Georgian architecture, is displayed by the four chimneys that stand tall on the home's slate roof.

The home's stunning design needs no elaborate decorations. Bordered by a row of tulip poplars, the sprawling manicured lawn also includes trees with historic significance. The east lawn's English yew is rumored to have been planted by George Washington, while a pecan tree on the west lawn was planted by none other than President Woodrow Wilson. Spectacular river views also include the opportunity to see America's national bird, the bald eagle. The area is a recognized breeding ground for these majestic creatures. Westover's river-side doorway boasts a pineapple, a sign of hospitality, which was replicated by other colonial plantations.

In 1761 William Byrd III remarried, and his new wife, Mary Willing, took over the plantation in 1777 after her husband's death. As tensions began to rise between the colonists and the royal government, the American Revolution broke out. Mrs. Byrd, who was a sympathizer to the colonist side, almost had a brush with the infamous Benedict Arnold. A general who formerly fought for the Continental army, Arnold's loyalties shifted after he married a Loyalist. In early January 1781, while leading British troops to Richmond, Arnold stopped at Westover to replenish horses and supplies. (Mr. Byrd was already dead.) Arriving in Richmond the next day, Arnold and his 1,600 men captured and burned the city to the ground.

Mrs. William Byrd III's estate sold Westover in 1817 to William Carter for $45,000. Exchanging hands often, Westover always remained privately owned. In 1999 Mrs. Bruce Crane Fisher, who had moved to Westover with her parents when she was 8, transferred her ownership to a household partnership where the plantation was managed by family members. In 2012 Andrea Fisher Erda and her husband, Rob, took over managing Westover.

Architecturally, the house hasn't undergone many changes, with the exception of modernizing the interior for plumbing and electricity. During the Civil War, Westover's east wing was destroyed by a fire, and when rebuilt was not done in the same fashion as the west wing. Five rooms are available to view: the Red Drawing Room, Green Drawing Room, Dining Room, East Wing, and Great Hall. Each have intricacies that tell the tale of Colonial history's ever-changing progression, one being the Rococo plasterwork seen throughout these rooms. Lighthearted in design, the French influence was all the rage in the mid-18th century, a departure from its heavy Baroque predecessor. The Rococo design can be seen in great detail around the ceiling, mantelpieces, and hanging light fixtures.

In the East Wing library, light pours in from the southern side of the home. Indigo blues and bright whites are alluring, while 19th-century portraits and paintings hang above fireplaces and along unspoiled walls. The Red Drawing Room is even cozier, with its black-marbled mantel and inviting window seats framed by striped crimson and cream cushions. Paisley patterned curtains draped on the windows create a homey but regal feel.

On the north side, a wrought-iron gate, considered the finest example from the 18th century, is flanked by six capped pillars symbolizing the plantation's ideology of virtue. The pineapple is repeated here, signifying hospitality. There is also an acorn for perseverance, a beehive for industry, an urn of flowers signifying beauty, a cornucopia for abundance, and a Greek key for knowledge. On the gate sits a pair of bald eagles with wings spread, ready to fly.

Leaving Westover may be the hardest part, but outside the home is where some of its best-kept secrets lie. A secret passageway was once used to escape from Indian raids along the riverbanks. Horses steal glances while walking to the barn, while blooms abound in the formal gardens. Here is where William Byrd I is buried. True to his character, Byrd's tombstone is quite elaborate, with a beautifully written epitaph whose inscription takes up both its north and south sides.

The Byrd name is one of the most influential lineages in Colonial Virginia as well as America due to the alliances the Byrd family made with other great early families such as the Carters and Harrisons, among others. Furthermore, their political clout in Virginia's early development as landowners was crucial to Colonial society. When the plantation passed out of the Byrd family, their legacy remained strong, as concurrent owners never let their presence be forgotten.

Westover is somewhat enchanted—with the chance to see a bald eagle flying overhead or a period movie being filmed on-site, there's never a dull moment. However, it is the James River that holds the most charm as it flows slowly past the house, lapping softly at its undisturbed banks. Countless ships and boats have viewed this magnificent architectural structure for over 265 years with little change to its facade. And if its ownership remains with those who guard its secrets with great care and attention, those special memories will continue to be formed.

Acknowledgments

Writing a book that features more than 40 plantations required assistance and cooperation from many, many people. Our deepest appreciation to the plantation owners, managers, workers, volunteers, and other officials who so graciously opened their doors and spent time with us. So many stories were shared along the way about the people who lived and worked in these mansions hundreds of years ago. We feel honored to have been afforded the opportunity to walk the grounds and hallways of these historic homes.

The three plantations considered the crown jewels—Mount Vernon, Montpelier, and Monticello—are watched over by stellar professionals who deserve special recognition for their dedication to preserving and educating visitors about the lives and times of our three Founding Fathers. At Mount Vernon, special thanks to Mary V. Thompson, research historian, and Dawn Bonner, manager of visual resources; at Montpelier, Giles Morris, vice president for communications and marketing, and Jeni Spencer, graphic designer; and, at Monticello, for the Thomas Jefferson Foundation, Inc., Mia Magruder, marketing associate, and Madeleine Rhondeau, communications.

The owners of several plantations epitomized Southern hospitality, since these amazing mansions also serve as their homes. Special thanks to Andrea Erda at Westover Plantation, Tad Thompson at Tuckahoe, Michelle Darnell at Belle Grove Plantation Bed & Breakfast, Brian Gordineer at Piney Grove at Southall's Plantation, and William W. Richardson III at Chelsea Plantation.

Along the way, various docents and guides provided exceptional tours. They include Julian Charity at Shirley Plantation, Clarence Harrison at Berkeley Plantation, Betsy Hanmer at Patrick Henry's Red Hill Plantation, Jessica Powers at Weston Plantation, and Kathryn Lane at Chippokes Plantation. Several plantations are owned and operated by the National Park Service, and their officials were knowledgeable and accommodated our requests. Special shout-outs to John Hennessy, the chief historian for the Fredericksburg and Spotsylvania National Military Park, whose insights about Chatham Manor and Ellwood Manor were invaluable; Emmanuel Dabney, curator for the Petersburg National Battlefield, who truly cares about the future of Appomattox Manor; and Jeffrey L. Nichols, president and CEO of Poplar Forest.

We would like to acknowledge the National Society of the Colonial Dames in the Commonwealth of Virginia, whose hard work and dedication have benefitted the Wilton House Museum, and Jennifer Hurst-Wende, at Preservation Virginia, whose passion is evident in the many properties that are watched over by this important organization. A huge thank-you to Tammy Higgs from Sully Historic Site and Mary Kesler from Poplar Forest, both of whom provided enriching as well as informative slave tours, separate from the main tour.

Thanks to our agent, Anne Marie O'Farrell, who first reached out to us about interesting topics in Virginia. Thanks also to our editor at Globe Pequot, Amy Lyons, who recognized the value of this book, telling the stories of these plantations in a new environment to a new audience.

Finally, to our families, who visited some of these plantations with us and shared our enthusiasm for this project.

—Jai Williams and Charlene Giannetti

Historical Trails: Follow in the Footsteps of Our Founders

There's an educational and fun way to learn more about the plantations featured in this book—by actually walking along the trails where historic events took place. The Road to Revolution highlights the key places leading up to the American Revolution, while the Virginia Civil War Trails explores more than 2,000 military events that happened in Virginia during that conflict. Virginia's contribution to America's birth and evolution spans over 400 years. So walk, discover, and enjoy!

THE ROAD TO REVOLUTION HERITAGE TRAIL: HTTP://ROADTOREVOLUTION.COM

Freedom from British rule along with pursuing individual freedoms made the original colonies a breeding ground for nationalistic ideologies that went on to spur the birth of a nation. The Road to Revolution Heritage Trail, through the interior and coastal lands of Virginia, highlights the places and the people involved in the Revolutionary War. Stops along the trail include Colonial Williamsburg; Ash-Lawn Highland, home of James Monroe; Gunston Hall; Thomas Jefferson's Monticello; James Madison's Montpelier; two of Patrick Henry's homes, Scotchtown and Red Hill; and, of course, George Washington's Mount Vernon.

THE VIRGINIA CIVIL WAR TRAILS: WWW.VIRGINIA.ORG/CIVILWARTRAILS

"Ready . . . Aim . . . Fire!" Although you won't hear those words while exploring Virginia's rural countryside, a few of these battles transpired not too far from some of the homes featured. During the five years that the Civil War raged on, each passing year troops on both sides traveled, camped, and fought throughout the state. In 1862 the Peninsula Campaign brought Confederate General John Magruder to the area where Endview Plantation and Lee Hall Mansion were built. That same year, President Lincoln visited Liberia Plantation, just a few miles from where the First Battle of Bull Run was fought. Battlefields in Fredericksburg and the Wilderness Battlefield include the plantation homes of Chatham and Ellwood, used as headquarters where commanders conferred on military strategy and hospitals where doctors, nurses, and volunteers tended to wounded soldiers.

Index

Federal style, 21, 34, 40, 44, 67, 71,
  84, 159
Ferry Farm, 24, 27, 136
Fisher, Mrs. Bruce Crane, 231
Fitzhugh, Anne Randolph, 2
Fitzhugh, William, 2, 9
Flemish bond brickwork, 14, 21,
  38, 67, 84, 125, 138, 148, 175,
  225, 228
Floyd, James John, 170
Floyd, John, 170
Forest, VA, 47
Fredericksburg, VA, 2
Freedman's Bureau, 196
French and Indian War, 26, 78
Fry, Colonel Joshua, 78
Fry, Henry, 78

G
Gardiner, David, 211
General Grant's HQ, 55
Georgian style, 2, 14, 21, 34, 55, 74,
  121, 122, 125, 141, 183, 196,
  212, 231
ghosts, 46, 193, 213, 231
Gilliam, Christian Eppes, 122
Gilliam, William, 122
Gilmer, William, 72
Gloucester, VA, 145
Gordineer, Joan, 208
Gordineer, Joseph, 208
Gordon, David, 143
Gothic Revival style, 56, 190

Granger, George, Sr., 90
Granger. Isaac, 90
Grant, General Ulysses S., 10, 59
Greaves, Lieutenant Colonel Fielding
  Lewis, 148
Greaves, Nellie Taylor, 148
Greek Revival style, 44, 67, 212
Gunston Hall, 14

H
Haight, Amy, 36
Haight, Jacob, 36
Hanger, James Edward, 208
Hankins, John Henry, 177
Hankins, Louisiana, 177
Harrison, Anne Carter, 180
Harrison, Benjamin, 180, 190, 198
Harrison, Benjamin, II, 180
Harrison, Benjamin, III, 180
Harrison, Benjamin, IV, 180
Harrison, Benjamin, V, 182, 190, 208
Harrison, Carter Bassett, 200
Harrison, Collier, 200
Harrison, Robert, 200
Harrison, William Henry, 182, 209
Harwood, Grace, 195
Harwood, Humphrey, 195
Harwood, Major William, Sr., 196
Harwood, Sir Edward, 195
Harwood, Thomas, 195
Harwood, Thomas F., 208
Harwood, Thomas, Jr., 195
Harwood, William, 195

Hemings, John, 49
Hemings, Sally, 49, 90
Hennessy, John, 4, 10
Henry, Dorothea Dandridge, 105, 113
Henry, Patrick, 103, 111
Henry, Sarah Shelton, 105, 113
Henry, William Wirt, 106
Hercules (Washington slave), 27
Herold, David, 133
Hertle, Eleanor Daughaday, 19
Hertle, Louis, 19
Highgate, VA, 227
Hill, Captain Edward, 215
Hill, General A. P., 204
Hill, Hannah Aston, 215
Hinds, William, 77
Hipkins, John, 132
Historic Avenel, 44
Historic Kittiewan, 198
Hooe, Rice, 198
Hooker, John Palmer, 134
Hooker, Mary, 134
Hopewell, VA, 55, 122
Horner, William E., 55
Hughes, John A., 208
Hutter, Edward Sixtus, 52
Hutter, Emma Cobbs, 52

I
Indian Massacre of 1622, 185
Ingalls, General Rufus, 59
Inn at Meander Plantation, The, 78
Italianate architecture, 203

About the Authors

Jai Williams is a writer and photographer whose work appears on the award-winning website Woman Around Town, as well as on NBC4, the Library of Congress, and Vice (Munchies) to name a few. Two of her photographs were selected for an exhibit at the Washington Historical Society, *For the Record: Artfully Historic D.C.*, where "50 Most Endangered Places in D.C." were highlighted. Her photographs can be seen in two books from Globe Pequot, *Discovering Vintage Washington, DC* and *New York's One-Food Wonders: A Guide to the Big Apple's Unique Single-Food Spots*.

After graduating from Texas A&M University, Jai moved to Virginia to further her education as well as her career. Always fascinated with the history of plantations, Jai often spends her weekends touring these historic homes while traveling and submersing herself in the experiences of those who lived and worked there. Bringing her viewpoint to *Plantations of Virginia* is not only a labor of love, but also a chance to raise awareness of those plantations with uncertain futures but still many stories left to be told.

Charlene Giannetti, editor of Woman Around Town, is the recipient of six awards from the New York Press Club for articles that have appeared on the website. A graduate of Syracuse University's S.I. Newhouse School of Public Communications, Charlene began her career working for a newspaper in Pennsylvania, then wrote for several publications in Washington, covering environment and energy policy. In New York, she was an editor at *Business Week* magazine, and her articles have appeared in many newspapers and magazines, including the *New York Times*.

Charlene is the author of 12 nonfiction books, 8 for parents of young adolescents written with Margaret Sagarese, including *The Roller-Coaster Years*, *Cliques*, and *Boy Crazy!* She and Margaret have been keynote speakers at many events and have appeared on the *Today Show*, *CBS Morning*, FOX News, CNN, MSNBC, NPR, and many others. Her new book is *Parenting in a Social Media World*. Charlene divides her time between homes in Manhattan and Alexandria, Virginia. After coming to Virginia, Charlene became fascinated with the state's history, and she and her husband have spent many weekends touring historic homes, including several plantations. Those visits sparked her interest in writing *Plantations of Virginia*.